What people are saying about *Getting to My Enough* ...

Marie grew up in a complex childhood filled with emotional and physical trauma including sexual abuse, divorce and abandonment, and family dysfunction. Marie's resilience and determination are powerful as she moves through life's challenges and reconciles her past, learns to accept and embrace herself, and rises to success personally and professionally. Her voice and insight provide a candid picture of how family can both destroy you and drive you 'to do better and be better'. Ultimately, Marie's faith and fortitude prevail as she overcomes trauma and cascading obstacles to rebuild, thrive, and positively impact lives through her service to the community.

— Traci Tomilli, MBA

Marie has authentically and thoughtfully opened her life to us in a way that will give everyone a reason to reflect and find inspiration in ourselves and others. The challenges we face in life can often be a source of strength and a cause for perseverance. The key is to use our experiences to grow rather than languish. Here is a quote from Michael Josephson that seems fitting: "Don't let others define you. Don't let the past confine you. Take charge of your life with confidence and determination and there are no limits on what you can do or be."

— Susan Von Zabern, MPA

Getting to My Enough

A Story of Faith, Resilience, and Survival

A MEMOIR BY

Dr. Marie Melanie Brown Mercadel

ISBN: 978-1-955622-52-3

Cover photography by: Portrait Creations Photography
Dave Frank

Published by
Fideli Publishing, Inc.
www.FideliPublishing.com

*For the strong and beautiful women
in the Brown family,
I want you to know that you are loved
and that you are enough.*

Table of Contents

The Beginning

This is Life

Becoming Dr. Marie

Note to Readers

Some portions of my memoir may include detailed descriptions that may relate to a situation that you or a loved one have encountered. Please be aware of any topics that may cause stress, shock, depression, or anguish while you are reading this book. You may find it necessary to read a little bit at a time to allow yourself to take a break and decompress before moving to the next chapter. You may also wish to consider the following suggestions:

- Speak to someone in your circle of support to discuss your thoughts.

- Skip the chapters that generate harmful memories.

- Keep a journal describing the passages that were upsetting to you. You might think about speaking to a therapist to discuss strategies for healing.

- Read the book at a time that does not interfere with your ability to sleep or work.

- If you need resources, please call the RAINN National Sexual Assault Telephone Hotline at 800-656-HOPE.

- If you have suicidal thoughts, please call the National Suicide Prevention Lifeline at 800-873-TALK.

Author's Message

My memoir is a straightforward depiction of my journey, the content is not colorful, and it may not be entertaining, but it is reflective of my reality. I am aware that my version of events may differ from that of some individuals who are mentioned in this book. It is not my intention to hurt or malign any person; therefore, some names have been changed to ensure anonymity.

I am determined to live in my truth and share my perspective related to my process and the ups and downs of my life. I have forgiven those who have hurt me, and I humbly ask for forgiveness from any person whom I may have hurt. I have spent parts of my life plagued by a lack of confidence, guilt, and shame for things that happened to me, some of which were within my control and others of which were not.

Through the course of writing my memoir, I didn't realize that my recollection of events would produce a cornucopia of emotions, including fear, embarrassment, anxiety, and anger. I have been in a constant battle with my psyche to allow myself the room for authenticity and transparency. My sincere desire is that my testament to survival may serve as a motivator for others who are on the path to recovery.

Healing is intentional. Living is intentional. Forgiveness is intentional. Self-love is one of the best gifts that one may accept for themselves.

My goal is to live the remainder of my years happy, positive, and peaceful. I will do so by being patient and kind to myself.

Foreword

Dr. Marie and I share a sisterly bond that will last a lifetime. Over the years, she has become an advisor, a supporter, a confidant, and a trusted friend. While reading her memoir, you will have an opportunity to see her transform her life and overcome traumatic events that could have prevented her from getting *to her enough*. The many layers and intersections of Dr. Marie's background will grip your heart and keep you engaged, while tapping into areas of your own expe-riences that may have been left dormant.

Dr. Marie takes an audacious and courageous leap of faith to write this memoir. My hope is that her efforts will encourage others who may have been silenced to speak their truth. Be prepared to cry and rejoice as she finds her inner voice and embraces the next phase of her life. This memoir is especially relevant today for women who seek to heal from societal and generational trauma.

One of my favorite Bible scriptures is Proverbs 31:8-9: *Speak up for those who cannot speak for themselves, for the rights of all who are desti-tute. Speak up and judge fairly; defend the rights of the poor and needy* (NIV). Thank you, Dr. Marie, for your transparency and giving permis-sion to others to break the chains of dysfunction that threaten to bind our families for years to come.

All Of My Love,
Dr. Vonda Rogers

The Beginning

CHAPTER ONE

A Childhood Interrupted

Take pride in how far you have come.
Have faith in how far you will go.
But don't forget to enjoy the journey.

~ Michael Josephson

My most prominent childhood memories involve the molestation that I suffered at the hands of my older brother, Edward. One instance stands out in my mind. On a freezing January morning in 1971, I recall lying stretched out on the floor in the bathroom on the cold blue and white tile in my parent's home, staring at the ceiling while Edward straddled me. The lingering smell of bleach from the freshly cleaned toilet invaded my nostrils when he pushed me down alongside the bathtub.

"No, stop it! I don't like it when you touch me between my legs and put your thing in my private parts, it hurts. My stomach aches on the inside when you do that to me." I tried to shove Edwards' body off mine, but my attempts were futile due to the heaviness of his body.

"Don't worry about it, the pain will go away soon. I'm going to make you feel special and I know that you will like it. I'm almost done anyway," Edward said.

I felt a throbbing sensation between my legs, and I believed that my insides were ripping apart. Too scared to cry out or to move, my body froze as though I existed in a state of paralysis.

I prayed for a knock on the door by my dad, my mom, my sisters, or my other brothers. I wanted him to stop. We always seemed to have a house full of people; yet not one person in the house was there to rescue me.

It wasn't the first time that Edward, my 18-year-old brother molested me. At seven years old, I knew that he should not kiss me, touch me, and put his hands all over my body. I silently screamed out for help, but the words floated around in my mind and never escaped my lips. I imagined drowning in a sea of nausea, confused as to why Edward would hurt me instead of protecting me, as brothers were supposed to do.

After what seemed like an eternity, Edward groaned as his hips moved up and down, and he released a milky, white, hot fluid that squirted out between my legs. When Edward finished, he wiped away the fluid with a tissue, cleaned the floor with that same tissue, and threw it in the toilet. I hated him touching me. I didn't like that wet, nasty stuff on any part of my body.

"You better not tell momma or daddy; they will be mad, and we are going to get a whipping. Stand up. Don't forget. You better keep quiet."

Why will I be whipped? When Edward touches me and puts his thing between my legs, it hurts so bad. However, I did keep quiet, believing that I might be blamed for letting my brother touch me and take off my clothes. I convinced myself that he would tell my parents about all the times that he had molested me in the bathroom, and the other places in which he seemed to trap me when we were alone.

A few minutes after we dressed and straightened our clothes, we left the bathroom.

"Melanie, what are you doing?" my older sister, Gwen, who preferred to use my middle name, called out to me from the front of the house.

I was sure that Gwen yelled my name because she wanted me to complete a chore or run an errand. As I appeared before her, I couldn't help but wonder where she had been five minutes earlier while my brother hurt me in the bathroom. Of course, I didn't dare pose that question. Edward passed by us in the hallway as we spoke and gave me a menacing glare behind Gwen's back.

I didn't share the abuse with my sisters, Gwen, Joyce, and Mary. I didn't think that they would believe me. I was a child and Edward was almost a grown man, being eleven years older than I am. My parents always stressed that we should respect our older siblings, so I adhered to that expectation. Outside of the areas where the abuse occurred, I continued to interact with my brother around the house as if the violations of my body did not exist.

Through dealing with more than three years of sexual abuse by a person whom I should have been able to trust, I learned how to hold in my emotions, mask my pain, and present a positive outlook to the world that indicated that life was good. The damaging approach to managing my reactions and having my voice silenced as a child took up residence in my mind as I dragged myself into adulthood.

Today I am more amazing
than I was yesterday.
And tomorrow
I will be downright awesome.

CHAPTER TWO

Meet the Browns

> *Generational dysfunction*
> *is cast upon the unborn, the unsuspecting,*
> *and the unprepared.*
>
> ~ Dr. Marie Brown Mercadel

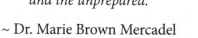

My mom, Ernestine, was an attractive, curvaceous, intelligent woman with a brown complexion, a bright smile, and a warm personality. People were drawn to her sunny disposition, and she had friendships with a diverse group of people from all walks of life. Born in 1937 in Albany, Georgia, to her mother, Lillie Mae, a domestic worker, and her father, Ernest, a laborer, she was raised in a modest house on Cottonwood Avenue surrounded by close-knit neighbors who lived by the motto that *it takes a village to raise a child.*

The union between my grandparents was short-lived, and they divorced when my mom attended elementary school. I have no memory of meeting my grandfather. My mom lived with Lillie Mae, and neighbors often cared for her when my grandmother's employer required her to work long hours.

After my grandparents divorced, my grandfather remarried, and his new wife gave birth to three children, two girls, and a boy. For unknown reasons, my mom didn't remain in frequent contact with her siblings or her dad. My mom seldom mentioned my grandfather, and no evidence existed that her parents maintained any level of communication once they divorced.

My mom gave birth to her first son, Edward, in June of 1953 when she was just 15 years old. With the help of my grandmother, she cared for Edward while she completed her high school studies.

My dad, Arthur, a short, handsome, chocolate-skinned, well-built young man with an imposing physique, was born in 1925 in Savannah, Georgia, to Laura and Walter Brown Sr. His sisters, Mary, Anne, Bernice, and Ruth were also born during this union. My father seldom spoke about his childhood, but I knew that he was raised in harsh living conditions. During this period in the South, families were plagued by poverty and struggled to buy essential items such as clothing, shoes, or enough food to meet the needs of the family.

My paternal grandparents divorced when my dad was eight years old, and my dad and his siblings faced the agony of being abandoned by their mother and their father. According to my cousin, my grandmother had a nervous breakdown and did not have the capacity to take care of her children. My paternal great-grandmother, Georgia Brown, took my dad and his siblings in and raised them to adulthood. During this time my dad and his siblings had infrequent contact with my grandfather. My grandfather later remarried, and he and his wife, Ethel, had four children, one boy and three girls.

Out of a desire to serve his country and improve his living circumstances, my dad enlisted in the United States Marine Corps in 1942 at the age of 17. He was assigned to a segregated training base named Montford Point, in Jacksonville, North Carolina. After President Harry Truman signed an executive order in 1948 to desegregate the Marine Corps, my dad transferred to the Marine Corps Logistics Base in Albany,

Georgia. My mom and dad met in Albany in 1953. At 16 years old, my mom began dating my dad, a 28-year-old sergeant.

I do not know if my dad initially knew about the twelve-year age difference between the two when he first met my mom or if he expressed concern about her status as a minor. Their age difference became an important factor in the demise of their relationship down the road.

My parents married after dating for six months. The birth of my sister Gwen followed less than a year later in 1954. In rapid succession between 1955 and 1958, my siblings Joyce, Arthur Jr., and Mary were born in Albany, Georgia.

In 1960 my dad transferred from his assignment in Albany to serve at Camp Lejeune, the military base in Jacksonville, North Carolina. I was born in 1964, four years after my parents arrived in North Carolina, followed by my younger brother Patrick in 1968. At the age of 31, my mom had given birth to seven children.

When my parents initially relocated to Jacksonville, Edward remained in Albany with my grandmother because she had been his primary caregiver since his birth. My mom spent much of her life as a young adult rearing her children without the opportunity to follow her own educational or career interests.

After serving in the military for eight more years, my father retired from the Marine Corps and decided to remain in Jacksonville, North Carolina, to raise his family. My mom worked part-time as a bus driver and a waitress, and my dad worked for a company that hauled lumber for contractors. According to my sister Mary's account, my parents devoted their time to raising their children, working, and attending church services on a weekly basis.

Your life doesn't have to be perfect to be meaningful,
but first you must understand the meaning of who
and what you are before you can live.

CHAPTER THREE

Mom, What Happened?

*The marks that humans leave
are too often scars.*

~ John Green

T he hustle and bustle of Saturday mornings often involved chores, music, chatter, laughter, and the smell of eggs, bacon, biscuits, grits, sausages, and pancakes cooking in the kitchen. The eight hundred-square-foot home seemed to swell with activity when my siblings and parents roamed about. By the time my dad retired from the Marine Corps in 1968, Edward had moved to Jacksonville to reside with us. Nine people lived in a three-bedroom, one-bath rental house.

All of the boys, Edward, Junior, and Patrick shared a bedroom at the front of the house, while Gwen, Joyce, Mary, and I bunked together in one bedroom in the middle of the house, and my parents slept in the bedroom at the back of the house.

One Saturday morning in the spring of 1971, my mom wasn't cooking breakfast when I woke up, and this seemed rather odd. She stayed in her bedroom for most of the morning, and I assumed that she had decided to sleep late. I had woken up early to clean my room because my godparents, Mr. and Mrs. Walter, usually picked me up on Saturday mornings.

When I darted into my mother's room to hug her before I left, she told me that she loved me and to have fun.

"Mom, are you alright?" I shuffled from one foot to the other.

She hugged me. "Yes, baby. I'm fine."

I brushed off my worries and skipped to the door to see my godparents.

Mr. and Mrs. Walter were longtime friends of my dad's, and they didn't have any children of their own. For some reason, they had taken a liking to me and brought me gifts, toys, and clothing for my birthday, Easter, and Christmas.

I looked forward to spending time with them every week; we purchased our favorite ice cream and watched the ducks at the park. The time that I spent with my godparents was special to me because in a house full of children it proved to be difficult to have any alone time or privacy. I also knew that for these few hours a week I could relax and avoid being around Edward.

We always drove through the car wash before Mr. and Mrs. Walter brought me home. I loved seeing the soapy water running down the windows. Watching the streaming water calmed me, even as a kid.

I enjoyed our outings, but I was anxious to return home so that I could see my mom. She had appeared sad when I left, and I wanted to check in on her. For some reason, it seemed as though Mr. and Mrs. Walter moved slowly and didn't want to take me home right away.

When we drove up to the house I hopped out of the car. My godparents followed behind me as I opened the front door.

I shouted as I ran inside, "Mom, I'm back."

To my alarm, my mom sat on a stool in front of a mirror in the living room washing blood off her face and holding an ice pack in her hand.

Her eyes were red, and I noticed the bruises, scratches, and the swelling on her face and torso. She looked like she had been in a brawl. As I watched her clean her wounds, my thoughts were racing, and I tried to figure out how she had received these injuries.

I sobbed as I watched her, confused. "Mom, what happened? Who did this to you? Where is Daddy?"

She hugged me and whispered, "I'm okay."

My godmother tried to pull me away from my mom, but I kicked and screamed, and she could not hold me back. I didn't understand what had taken place. I had never seen my mom in this condition.

My sister Gwen helped my mom put an ice pack on the bruises on her back. I could tell that Gwen was angry and frightened. Her body shook, and her eyes welled with tears. I became scared and my heart pounded because I didn't know how my mom had come by the ugly welts that formed on her body. As the baby girl, a momma's girl, I needed to know what had happened.

Soon after I arrived home, my sister Joyce and my brother Junior had come into the house. Both remained quiet as they surrounded my mom and held her hands. I felt helpless; I didn't know how to make my mom feel better.

I grew overwhelmed, I knew that my mom was hurt, and I wanted my dad to make the situation better. I went to look for him, and he wasn't anywhere in the house. Nothing made sense. In my mind I thought that my dad should have been there to protect my mom.

After my mom was cleaned up, she lay down in her bed, and I crawled under the covers next to her. I refused to leave her side. Patrick snuggled in behind me and squeezed me. We held onto each other in silence.

I stared at the ceiling for what seemed like hours. As darkness crept in through the windows, I heard my dad return. He remained in the living room for the rest of the evening. Gwen stood watch and continued to come into the room to observe my mom. Finally, we dozed off, and Patrick and I slept with my mom for the entire night.

On Sunday, my siblings stayed in the house for most of the day. The air was still and tense and absent of the usual laughter and teasing between us. The rift between my parents was obvious, and I could see that my dad tried to comfort my mom and that she resisted his attempts to communicate with her.

The next day I realized that the bruises that my mom had suffered were as a result of an altercation with my dad. I had never heard my parents argue, raise their voices, or have any type of disagreement. It never occurred to me that my dad and mom would get into an argument, let alone a physical fight.

CHAPTER FOUR

Where is She?

> *In the process of letting go,*
> *you will lose many things from the past,*
> *but you will find yourself.*
>
> ~ Deepak Chopra

On the Monday morning following that anxiety-filled weekend, I woke up to organize my supplies for school, just like any other day. The atmosphere remained tense, but my mom seemed to be moving around better, and the swelling on her face had gone down. My dad left for work at his usual time, and my siblings ran around in different stages of preparing for school. We all hustled out of the house to start our day, and I remember giving my mom an extra long hug. I expected to see her later in the evening.

The elementary school that I attended, Clyde Erwin, was less than a mile from our house, and I often walked to school. Most days my friends Wanda and Panessa, two sisters from the neighborhood, joined me, and we laughed and talked so much on our way to class that sometimes we ended up being late to school. My day was uneventful, and I thought about my mom a lot. As soon as the bell rang, I exited the classroom so that I could make my way home.

My older sister Gwen always arrived home before I did, and she greeted me at the front door. I stepped inside and placed my books on the table.

"Did you have a nice day?" Gwen squeezed my shoulder.

"Yes, what time is mom coming home from work?"

Gwen ignored my question, and I grew fearful.

My siblings arrived home from school and attended to their homework. Later, my dad entered the house through the back door with my brother Patrick in tow. My entire family was accounted for except for my mom. The afternoon vanished in favor of the darkness of the night.

It was almost my bedtime, and I continued to wait for my mom. Usually, she made it home from her waitressing job in time to tuck me into bed. As the hands on my watch approached nine o'clock pm, I waited for her to walk through the front door. The door never opened, and I knew something was wrong.

"Where is she? Is Mom working late?" I pleaded for an answer.

Neither my dad nor my siblings seemed to be able to give me a reply as to when my mom would be home for the night.

My brother Patrick and I fell asleep on the couch waiting for her to arrive. At some point during the night Gwen put us to bed.

For the next week I woke up and repeated the cycle. I looked for my mom each morning before I left for school. I ran home from school each day and prayed that she would be there. After what seemed like endless days of waiting for my mom to return home, I finally realized that she would not be back, at least not any time soon.

My dad did his best to make it seem as though our lives were normal without my mom in the house. It was rare for him to show his emotions, and he tried hard to reassure us kids that we would be okay.

As I had followed my mom's every move on the previous Sunday, I wish that I had known that in the next forty-eight hours she would leave me behind. Almost two years passed before my siblings and I saw our mom again, a two-year gap that seemed more like a century. The time that I spent wondering where my mom was created a pit in my stomach that would remain throughout my childhood.

Before you can give your best self to the world
you must first pause and ensure that you are
practicing self-care.
Pay yourself first, don't give it all away.

CHAPTER FIVE

My New Abnormal

*Every flower must grow
through the dirt.*

~ Kristen Duke

Two months after my mom left, I overheard my sisters Gwen and Joyce discussing the fact that she had moved to Rialto, California, with the assistance of some of her friends. They also spoke about Gwen helping my mom pack her clothes after the rest of us left for school. I remained quiet, and they were unaware that I overheard the conversation.

To this day I still do not know all the details about why she chose California or how she traveled there and found a place to live and a job. We never discussed with whom she left, and most important, why she made the decision to leave my siblings and me behind.

I believe that my mom knew that my dad had the financial means to raise us, as she had primarily been a stay-at-home mom, part-time waitress, and school bus driver during the marriage. I also believe that my mom viewed herself as being trapped in a way. She had a high school diploma but at that point had never attended college.

As I look back, I realize that she must have felt stressed out and ill-equipped to parent all seven of her children as a single mom. Her childhood had been cut short by the birth of Edward, and she grew up alongside her babies. It wasn't until I was in my late teens that I learned from my sister Joyce that Edward had a different father, a revelation that shocked me.

We never used the term *half* in my house, and my dad treated Edward like his own child. For this reason, Edward remained in the household when my mom moved to California.

After my mom left, we settled into a routine, with Gwen serving as the de facto matriarch of the family. At 17 years old, Gwen's role evolved to the most trustworthy and responsible child among all of us. She had a gruff personality, but she was kind and caring and always ready to help a person in need. Gwen and I were ten years apart, and I always viewed her as more of a mother figure than a sister. She played a key role in my life.

Gwen and my mom had a close bond, and my mom's departure brought about a schism in their relationship. On one hand, Gwen helped my mom leave so that she could protect her. On the other hand, the sparkle disappeared from Gwen's eyes on the day that my mom left. She assumed the role of a 17-year-old in charge of nurturing children during a time when she should have been contemplating the next steps in her life.

Adding to her stress as the oldest sister, at the age of 17 Gwen gave birth to her own child, Pamela, in October of 1971, the same year that my mother left for California. Girls need their mothers in the same way that boys need their fathers. Without my mom present in the house, I felt lost in the shuffle amid all of my siblings as we tried to figure out what to do next.

I loved my dad, and I admired his courage and sacrifices. He could have walked away and went on with his life without his kids, but he didn't. I believe that he understood the torment of being abandoned by his own parents as a child, and for this reason he wanted to keep us together as a family.

My unusual home environment contributed to my feelings of being an outsider who didn't belong. The fact that my dad raised me made me different from most of my peers.

The role of a single dad had to be demanding, but my dad made his best effort to give us a stable home. Perhaps we did not have the material items that we wanted, but we had what we needed.

I wish that I would have understood some of the worries and fears that my dad must have faced as a single father who had seven children and a granddaughter to support. Maybe then my teenage behavior would have been less defiant.

Over time, the line of communication opened between my mom and my dad, and she advised him that she wanted to end the marriage. Even though my mom informed my dad that she desired to live on her own and wanted to focus on obtaining her nursing degree, I believe that he always thought that she would return home to her family.

My mom insisted that she would participate in our upbringing and maintain involvement in our lives to the extent possible. While my mom never had an intimate relationship with my dad again, they never signed a formal separation agreement or filed for divorce. They maintained most of their joint accounts, credit cards, and insurance policies. When my dad purchased our home, the deed was titled in both of their names. My parents reconciled enough of their differences that they could be amicable and committed to co-parenting long distance.

My parents spoke often, and my dad consulted with my mom about the major events that arose in our lives. The course of adjusting to our atypical existence without our mom in the house was hard for all of us kids. Speaking to her by telephone did little to ease my longing to hug and kiss her and to have her tuck me into bed. I still had a mom, but the lone-liness persisted and was accompanied by sadness and a sense of being deserted. As a young girl I did not know how to express the emotions that I suppressed because of the major life change that I experienced.

There was not an item of clothing, a vacation, a toy, or a favorite show that filled the void of losing my mom. My siblings and I each dealt with the hurt in our own way.

At times I reflect on the sorrow in myself as a child, and I see now how each of my siblings reacted to my mom's absence in our lives. As we grew older and faced our own problems, the negative effect of her departure contributed to the poor decisions we made about life, love, and relationships. When there isn't a healthy example to follow, it is hard to make sterling decisions related to the various circumstances that are a regular part of life.

CHAPTER SIX

Let's Pretend
We are a Real Family

Bear with each other and forgive one another.
If any of you has a grievance against someone,
forgive as the Lord forgave you.

~ Colossians 3:13

By 1973, my mom had found a permanent job as an administrative assistant, leased an apartment, and saved money to purchase a car. She had also enrolled in a part-time licensed vocational nursing program. As she settled in and created a new life for herself in California, her goal was for my siblings and me to visit her during our annual summer breaks from school. After checking into the price of plane tickets, she realized that she could not afford to purchase plane tickets for seven children.

Since the goal of flying us to California could not be achieved, my mom requested that my dad allow her to come to our home and spend four weeks with us kids each year. My dad agreed.

She managed to arrange the time off with her employer; sometimes her visits were during the summer and other times the visits were during the school year. We always anticipated her arrival, and my siblings talked about the enjoyable activities that we could do together as a family.

At my dad's direction, prior to my mom's arrival each year we launched into a deep cleaning mode that encompassed scrubbing walls and floors from top to bottom, organizing the bedrooms, cutting the grass, pulling the weeds, and washing the windows. My dad wanted the house to be neat when my mom arrived.

For the most part, on a typical day the house stayed orderly. When my siblings and I woke up we immediately made our beds. We didn't leave dishes in the sink or put pots and pans in the refrigerator. When we finished playing with toys, we stored them in the closet. Due to my dad's military background, he instilled in us the importance of keeping our belongings tidy and arranged in their proper place.

Each week my sisters and I rotated the chore assignments, and my brothers managed the tasks in the yard. Nevertheless, we all went above and beyond in anticipation of my mom's stay.

While she was in town during the school year my mom attended parent/teacher conferences. She cooked our favorite meals and we also watched television, shopped, and played games. We interacted as any typical family would, except we knew that her time with us would be brief and that she would go away for several months until we saw her again. We played the role of an intact and functional family for thirty days out of the year.

The first year that my mom visited in 1973, I prayed that she would change her mind about going back to California or take me away from the abuse that I endured at the hands of Edward. Better yet, I longed for reconciliation between my mom and my dad. I envisioned us taking a new family portrait that would hang on the living room wall. When the reunion between my parents didn't happen, I internalized my anger.

Each year I planned to tell my mom about the incestuous liaisons that Edward forced upon me, but I always panicked and changed my mind. Knowing the importance of the time my siblings and I spent with her, I didn't want her visits to be ruined by my revelations of the abuse.

Edward stayed away from me when my mom was home. He didn't dare corner me in the bathroom or try to rub his body against mine. But he warned me in advance that he would be watching me and threatened to hurt me if I told my mom that he had sex with me.

The abuse had escalated, and Edward had increased the frequency of the molestation to twice a week. I wanted a childhood that was free from mistreatment and an escape from my anguish. I knew that what Edward did to me was wrong, and I started to believe that it was my fault.

My mom attempted to convince my dad to permit Patrick and me to return with her to California, but my dad refused. I felt like a pawn in an agonizing and dysfunctional game of chess. The trauma and stress that I developed from the sexual abuse and the loss of my mom's presence caused me to consider committing suicide.

Choose happiness.
Practice the 3Gs —
grace, gratitude, and greatness.
Fall down often and get back up
each and every time.
Throw the playbook away
and let things flow as they are destined.

CHAPTER SEVEN

Did He Touch You?

You may have had unfair things happen to you. But the depth of your pain is an indication of the height of your future.

~ Joel Osteen

I n the fall of 1973, my dad applied for and received a loan to have a new home built for my family in the Piney Green area of Jacksonville, North Carolina. The nine of us, my dad, my six siblings, and my niece Pam needed more space. The new, fourteen hundred-square-foot, four-bedroom house provided enough room for the entire family. We moved into the home during the middle of my fourth-grade school year in 1974 and my dad wanted me to finish out the term at my current school.

In the mornings my dad dropped me off at school. In the afternoon, I rode the bus to Mrs. Betty's house, a close family friend. She had four children, three girls, Jennifer, Melissa, and Jaclyn, and one boy, Jonathan. Mrs. Betty served us snacks and helped us with our homework, and afterwards we played outside while I waited for my dad to pick me up.

One day we played a game that we named *boyfriends and girlfriends*. We were all between the ages of 10 and 13, so none of us had a real-life boyfriend or girlfriend, but we liked to pretend that we were older. Jonathan, 13, played the role of my boyfriend. Once the game began, Jonathan cupped my face in his hands and tried to kiss me.

"Yuck"! I proclaimed and pushed him away from me. "Don't do that. My brother Edward does that to me. He always takes my clothes off."

My friends stared at me with bewildered looks on their faces. Suddenly, Jennifer darted inside the house, and I didn't realize that she alerted Mrs. Betty to what I told the other kids. We continued to play our game, me in a state of oblivion.

When my dad arrived to pick me up, he entered the house to say hello to Mrs. Betty. When he exited the front door and sat beside me on the porch, it seemed as though the blood had drained from his face. Though he had skin like Hershey's chocolate, at that moment his complexion seemed much lighter. I could tell that he was upset, and he remained silent for several minutes.

"Has Edward been touching you?"

I nodded.

"How long has this been going on?"

"It started in second grade".

I prayed that he would believe me and that I would not be whipped. My dad gently grabbed my hand, and we walked to the car. As we rode home, I spent the next twenty-five minutes leaning against the door in the back seat with my eyes closed and pretended to be asleep. My dad and I never spoke of this incident again.

Once we were home, I noticed that my dad took Edward into his bedroom to talk to him. The day after their discussion, Edward packed his personal belongings and left the house. I don't know with whom he left, and I never questioned my dad regarding his whereabouts. My siblings did not discuss his absence when I was present. I was relieved that he left, and I didn't care if he ever returned. I wish that I could say that he left permanently, but that was not the case.

My parents had countless conversations and my siblings were not always privy to the information they exchanged. I assumed at that time that my dad had a discussion with my mom about my brother and his abusive behavior toward me. I believed that they kicked him out of the house and sent him away.

More than fifteen years later, I learned that my dad did not divulge the molestation to my mom. Without a formal custody agreement, she could have taken any of her children without my dad's consent. This was likely one of his fears, and for this reason, I believe that my dad kept the molestation a secret.

Just because you are struggling
doesn't mean you are failing.
It is possible, but rare to achieve
all of your goals the first time around.
Allow your faith to be bigger than your fear,
keep striving each day to win,
don't give up.

CHAPTER EIGHT

Friends, Anyone?

Turn to me and be gracious to me,
for I am lonely and afflicted.

~ Psalm 25:16

At the beginning of the next school year, I attended Tabernacle Elementary School, where I started the fifth grade. Most of my classmates attended primary school together or knew each other from growing up in the same neighborhood. Unless a family moved to the community due to a military assignment, not many new kids moved to the area.

Each day at school seemed to last for fifty-three hours. I knew one person named Laura, whom I considered a friend. We sat across from each other in the back of the room for the two subjects that we had together. Outside of class she buddied around with her cousins.

At my new school, a group of four mean girls taunted me by throwing paper and spitballs at my head. They also liked insulting me and calling me ugly and skinny. I tried to evade them at all costs to avoid a physical fight. I imagined punching each of them in the eye, but the potential consequences of suspension from school or detention prevented me from acting. During lunchtime, I didn't have a companion to eat with, so I often spent my time in the library alone reading books.

Not all my classmates were mean to me, but I knew that I was different. They all had moms. Many of them even had moms and dads. I accepted my belief that my classmates were better than me since they had two parents. My lack of self-confidence also contributed to my awkwardness about ways to learn how to make friends in an unfamiliar learning environment.

I loved school, but I didn't have an eagerness to attend. Team sports, team games, or classroom assignments in which one had to have a partner increased my level of nervousness. Except for Laura, not one person in any of my classes wanted to be my partner. During my fifth-grade year, I contemplated developing a plan to ditch school after an embarrassing incident.

During science class before the Christmas break the teacher announced, "Okay, students, we are going to divide into two teams, and each team will be assigned a question about the elements in the periodic table. The winning team will be rewarded with ice cream sandwiches."

"Rebecca, you are the leader of team one. Donna, you choose the students for team two."

Twenty-five of us waited during the selection process. I grew more and more anxious as I eagerly anticipated hearing my name. Finally, I was the last person waiting. Neither Rebecca nor Donna called my name, a clear sign that they did not want me to join their teams. The teacher didn't notice, so I schlepped over to a team as though I belonged there. The sense of humiliation crushed me.

This slight from my classmates confirmed what my immature mind had thought all along. I didn't belong. My impression of being an outcast stayed in my consciousness. It is amazing how powerful our brains are and the way that we sometimes rely on single stories to influence our beliefs.

Three years later as an eighth grader I wanted to join the cheerleading team or the girls' basketball team, but due to the after-school practices and games I didn't have transportation home. Although my sisters all had cars, their work and school commitments conflicted with the athletic program at my school. My dad's work schedule often required late evening hours, so he was unavailable to pick me up either. I assumed that if I could be part of a group and make more friends, I would be more content.

I loved to read. To fight the loneliness, I buried myself in studying and reading on the weekends. I spent a lot of time, sometimes the entire day on Saturday and Sunday, in my bedroom with the door closed watching television, reading, drawing, writing, or listening to music. Today, I find solace in spending time alone with my inner thoughts.

From the lens of a child, I viewed the lives of my classmates as ideal. These people seemed self-assured, jovial, and cool. I convinced myself that the reason why my classmates were without problems was because their parents lived together.

It was interesting that as I grew older into my late teens and early twenties, at least six of the two-parent relationships in my neighborhood ended in separation or divorce. This fact represented my first lesson that things are not always as they seem when one is on the outside peering into a window of another person's life. At the time, however, I believed that my acquaintances lived in a secure, intact family, as opposed to me, who did not.

Don't let the success of others
lead you to feel like a failure.
Every person's journey is unique,
and what HE has for you will be for you
when the time is right.
Be patient. Be still. Be focused. Be determined.
Success is not a byproduct of wishes;
but rather a result of lessons,
determination, and perseverance.

CHAPTER NINE

Finally, a Reprieve

I keep my eyes always on the Lord.
With him at my right hand,
I will not be shaken.

~ Psalm 16:8

In 1978, at the beginning of my freshman year at White Oak High School, my brother Junior left for the Army, and Gwen, Joyce, Mary, Patrick, and I remained in the home. Halfway through the semester, Edward returned to live with us. He was 25 years old with a muscular build and his presence scared me.

At that time, I learned that after he moved out, he enrolled in a vocational skills training program in Louisville, Kentucky to study for his general education diploma and to learn a trade. When his time at the program ended, he gained employment in the construction field in Jacksonville.

I couldn't believe that my dad gave Edward permission to return home, but I remained quiet and didn't express my concerns. Nor did my dad check in with me to make sure that I was okay. The sense of comfort and safety that I had when Edward left disappeared, and I walked around the house with a heightened state of dread.

My dad might have hoped that Edward would not attempt to molest me or hurt me again. The assumption was incorrect. Edward's behavior remained unchanged, and he continued to try to corner me in various parts of the house.

However, at 14 years of age, I recognized that I needed to be assertive with him. I threatened to let my dad know that he tried to touch me. Although I had doubts that my defensive posture would work, he backed off when he realized that my fear of him had decreased. He left me alone, maybe because he worried that he would be exposed. He also might have been scared away after he discovered that I had started menstruating.

I silently questioned why my dad did not save me from my brother and I became resentful. I wish that he would have understood that having to live under the same roof with Edward again was traumatic. He obviously did not understand that the abuse that I suffered at the hands of my brother would have consequences related to my actions, thoughts, and behaviors for the rest of my life.

CHAPTER TEN

Melanie, Are You Pregnant?

For I reckon that the sufferings of this present time are worthy to be compared with the glory, which shall be revealed in us.

~ Romans 8:18

With Edward living in the house again, the bitterness I held in my heart increased. To try to avoid being around him as much as possible, after my freshman year of high school I volunteered as a candy-striper at Onslow Memorial Hospital during the summer. I worked on the weekends so that my dad or my siblings could provide transportation for me.

One of my responsibilities involved working at the front desk giving information to visitors and answering the phone. One weekend during that summer I met a boy named Kenneth when he stopped in to see a sick family member. He attended the same school as I did, but he lived in a different neighborhood. We had never crossed paths at school, although we knew some of the same people. We exchanged numbers and after that spoke on the telephone every night.

My dad did not approve of me having a boyfriend, so I kept Kenneth a secret from my family. I used my volunteer job as a candy-striper as a cover for my trips to meet Kenneth while his mother worked. I started manipulating my schedule so that he could pick me up and spend time with me, and I returned to the hospital before my designated pick-up time by a member of my family.

Kenneth and I had sexual intercourse and were too naïve to use condoms. When I missed my period two months in a row, we comprehended enough about sex to know that I was pregnant.

As 15-year-old high school sophomores, Kenneth and I didn't have the resources or the maturity level to raise a baby. I tried to hide the pregnancy for as long as I could. I turned on the shower to mask the sound when I vomited every morning. As expected, my five-foot, five-inch, one-hundred-and-ten-pound frame widened quickly, and my clothes tightened. Neither my siblings nor my dad noticed the changes in my body.

I had no idea how to deliver the news to my dad. I did not want to disappoint him because he already had so much on his plate. I also figured that my mom would also be livid. I don't know how I believed that I could hide the secret forever and praying each night that I would no longer be pregnant in the morning never worked.

I have a vivid recollection of my teacher notifying me that my sister Gwen wanted to see me in the front office of the school. I was in the middle of taking an English quiz when she excused me from class.

As I walked down the hallway, I spotted Gwen standing outside of the office door. The angry scowl on her face almost caused me to turn around and return to my class.

Gwen lost it when I faced her. "Melanie, tell me the truth? Are you pregnant?"

As I mentally tried to determine how she had found out, I knew that it would be useless to deny the facts. I nodded.

She instructed me to go back to class and declared that we would have a discussion once I arrived home.

As expected, I barely passed the quiz. Instead of concentrating on the test I thought about our exchange and Gwen's demeanor. In a way, relief washed over me because I needed help figuring out the next steps and how Kenneth and I could take care of a baby.

To my dismay, my dad, my mom, and Gwen had an advance conversation about my pregnancy before I arrived home. No discussion took place about what I wanted to do, including the option of raising the baby or placing it for adoption. Kenneth didn't have a say. My parents forbade him from coming to our home and refused to take his phone calls. Once they decided that I would have an abortion, Gwen scheduled the procedure for the following week.

On the morning of the appointment, Gwen signed me in at the clinic and informed me that she would be back in the afternoon.

When the medical assistant called my name, I entered a cold and sterile operating room. I undressed and lay down on a metal table waiting for the doctor to enter. I counted the tiles on the ceiling and nervously tapped my feet to the beat of the background music.

When the door opened and the doctor walked in, my body stiffened, and my tears started flowing. Fright and relief washed over me when he examined me and determined that at fifteen weeks pregnant, the dilation and curettage procedure could not be performed.

Initially I thought that this meant that the abortion would be cancelled. My hope was short lived. When Gwen returned to pick me up, she became agitated when the doctor explained that to safely terminate the pregnancy my labor needed to be induced and I would be required to deliver the baby at the hospital.

I will never forget lying on the table at the abortion clinic while the long needle pierced my belly button to insert the solution that would terminate the pregnancy. As I think about the sting of the liquid as it flowed through my body, my chest constricts, and tears form in my eyes even now.

Following the injection, Gwen drove me across the street to the hospital, signed the admission papers, and went home. Shortly after I arrived in my room, the sharp, stabbing labor pains commenced. For the next six hours I tossed and turned and writhed around the bed as the cramping intensified. The nurses drifted in and out of the room throughout the course of the evening to monitor my vital signs and check my cervix.

After a severe contraction, a warm fluid gushed from my vagina. I placed my hands between my legs, and I felt the soft body of my baby. Depressed and alone, I gave birth to a stillborn daughter. Before I rang the call button to summon the nurse, I held her in my arms and cried for nearly an hour. Writing about the abortion evokes in me feelings of distress and torment. The abortion continues to shake me to this day.

I live with the shame and regret of being too weak to refuse to move forward with the procedure. The emotional and psychological trauma associated with having an abortion served as the precursor for much of the hurt that I attempted to soothe as I entered adulthood. If I had carried my baby girl to term, she would be 41 years old today.

I bore no anger toward Gwen for taking me to have an abortion. She did this with the full knowledge of both of my parents, and I believe that she wanted to give me a chance to graduate from high school and go to college. She missed that opportunity herself due to her involuntary role as mother to her six siblings as well as being a mother to her own daughter.

CHAPTER ELEVEN

California Bound

> *Take the path to a new beginning.*
> *I am always with you,*
> *and I will always love you.*
>
> ~ Dad

At the end of my sophomore year of high school in 1980, my mom used my abortion as leverage to convince my dad that I needed to relocate to California. He agreed that I could leave and that I would fly back with her at the end of the summer. Yet, he refused to agree to my younger brother Patrick coming with us. He was a 3-year-old toddler when my mom left, and at the age of 12 he also wanted to move.

I managed the competing emotions of joyfully fantasizing about living a glamorous life in California and dolefulness since I didn't want to depart without Patrick. My guilt extended to knowing that I would not see my siblings on a regular basis. Although they were adults and could have made the choice to move to California, they were engaged in living their own lives in North Carolina.

To further add to the sadness associated with moving three thousand miles away from my siblings, my dad became ill. One month prior to my scheduled flight, he received a diagnosis of chronic obstructive pulmonary disease (COPD) and congestive heart failure (CHF).

Throughout my childhood I had dreamed of moving to California. After learning of my dad's illness, my excitement for this impending adventure waned.

On the morning of our flight, I saw my dad become emotional for the first time in my life. He cried and hugged me for what seemed like hours. I no longer wanted to leave, and in that moment, if he had requested that I stay, I would never have boarded the plane.

He told me that he loved me, a rarity, and assured me that he would be fine and that he wanted me to leave so that I could be exposed to new opportunities.

Once we arrived in California and settled into our lives, my mom and I worked through the process of getting to know each other, since we hadn't lived in the same house for nine years.

As we spent time together, I needed my mom to understand that the soul of the 7-year-old little girl she had left behind in 1971 had changed. I bore the deep scars of sexual abuse, the memory of holding my still-born baby girl in my arms, and the bullying that I endured during my elementary school years, none of which were conducive to living a happy childhood.

I kept expecting my mom to bring up the sexual abuse and the abortion, but she didn't broach either subject. I didn't know it at the time, but multi-generational dysfunction and unresolved trauma played a role in the way that my mom and my dad parented my siblings and me and in the way that they addressed sensitive issues.

By the time I moved to California, my mom's financial situation had improved. She tried hard to make me comfortable. I loved the decorations in my room. I had my own television, a radio, and a telephone. We shopped together on the weekends, enjoyed eating at the Sizzler Restaurant, and watched an occasional movie at the theater.

However, sometimes we seemed to engage in a wordless battle that pitted her desire to raise me as a child against my desire for her to see that I was already beyond that point in my life. My mom loved me, and I loved her as well, but I was broken on the inside, and she lacked the ability to acknowledge that I had profound wounds that needed to be healed before our relationship could become closer.

I began my junior year at Eisenhower High School in Rialto, California. The school had more than five thousand students with a campus four times larger than it had been at my previous school in North Carolina. I looked forward to a different experience, but I missed my siblings and my dad. Transitioning from a house full of people who were always noisy to a quiet two-bedroom duplex was a culture change within itself.

I did well at Eisenhower. I met many people there from various ethnicities and backgrounds. Some of my classmates belonged to gangs, budding rap groups, modeled in fashion shows, and made appearances in music videos. Security guards patrolled each of the buildings at the school. I found this both scary and odd because we didn't need security at my school in North Carolina. The campus was open, which meant that students could leave during lunch and eat at the surrounding restaurants, or they could hang out on school grounds.

My social life improved, and some of the students who realized that I was new welcomed me. Of course, many established cliques and groups existed, but I met boys and girls with whom I could bond and build friendships.

During school registration I met a girl named Lena Stuckey. She became my lifelong friend and at one point spent a year living with my mom and me. We were more like sisters than friends. Spending time with her eased the emptiness that lodged in my heart without my sisters around.

Although I spent less than two years at Eisenhower, I have fond memories of my time there as a student. My mom encouraged me to join the tennis team, a dance team, and she gave me permission to participate in extracurricular activities. I liked attending football games, basketball games, and track meets.

After she worked her way through school and became a licensed practical nurse, my mom landed a position as the director of staff development at a skilled nursing facility. She had a knack for working with older adults and loved her job.

At her urging I became a volunteer during the summer and spring breaks during my time in high school. I assisted the residents of the facility by reading them stories, painting the fingernails of the ladies, and playing board games with them.

My devotion to public service and endangered populations started early in my life. Giving back to others has always created solace and a sense of peace for me.

During the time that I was in California, I spent a great deal of time talking to my dad on the telephone. In fact, we briefly spoke every day. I missed him terribly. Many of the conversations included my complaints about my mom. He listened but remained neutral so that he wouldn't step on my mom's toes. Never once did he disagree with her approach or her decisions. I could have worked harder at the relationship with my mom at the time, but I often thought about the day when I could move out on my own.

As a child I longed for the chance to live with my mom. When it had finally happened, it proved to be difficult for me to process the sense of abandonment that I absorbed as a child. I desperately wanted a mom and a dad, like many of the other families in my neighborhood.

Most of my anger was directed toward my mom. I understood that my dad had played a critical role in their separation, but it seemed as though I held my mom more responsible. I thought that she should have figured out how to develop a plan that kept our family together. It took time for me to mature and grow before I could reconcile the resentment that I carried in my heart.

Everyday

you have an opportunity

to be great.

CHAPTER TWELVE

I am Grown Up Now, Kind of

Life presents many choices.
The choices we make determine
our future.

~ Catherine Pulsifer

At the beginning of my senior year of high school, I learned that due to the number of class credits that I had earned prior to my transfer to Eisenhower High School, I could graduate mid-term in January of 1982. I spent months trying to convince my parents to allow me to move one hundred miles away to enroll in San Diego State University (SDSU).

My mom wanted me to go to a local school, and without the financial support of my parents, I could not afford the tuition to attend SDSU. I agreed to take courses at San Bernardino Valley College, a community college thirty minutes from where I lived in Rialto.

In high school I had grown enamored with the idea of becoming a military officer after I met a United States Air Force recruiter at the mall. I would need a bachelor's degree in order to pursue that option. I started classes at San Bernardino Valley College in March of 1982 with the goal of studying nursing and later earning a master's of science. My enrollment at the college led to an eleven-year journey to complete my undergraduate degree.

At first, I went with the flow and studied nursing because this met my mom's expectation. Even though I had spent four years working as a candy-striper and volunteering in a skilled nursing facility, I still wasn't sure that nursing would be the best profession for me. Nevertheless, I took the mandated prerequisites for obtaining an associate's degree.

I earned a B average during my first quarter in college. Learning new information and reading about research excited me. I remained unsure if I wanted to become a nurse, but I knew that the classes that I took would count toward any degree that I chose to pursue.

I developed a new sense of freedom and possessed confidence that I could make my own decisions about the next steps to take in my life. At the end of my second quarter, I weighed moving into my own apartment. I worked a part-time job, and I received four hundred dollars a month in disability benefits from the social security administration because my dad was unable to work. I believed that I could afford to live on my own. In anticipation of moving, I saved money from my job to pay for deposits, furniture, and utilities.

However, my third quarter was disastrous, I failed all but two of my classes. During school I had met a classmate who was an airman stationed at Norton Air Force Base, and I spent more time with him in the barracks than I did attending classes or studying. My mom assumed that I was going to classes as scheduled, and I didn't offer any information to the contrary or divulge that my grades had slipped.

To continue receiving the social security disability benefits, I needed to maintain full-time enrollment in school and earn a 2.5 grade point average. After the third quarter I lost my benefits, and the plan to move out evaporated before my eyes.

My mom found out about my grades when she read the letter of financial disqualification that arrived in the mail. When she confronted me with the letter, her voice quivered, and she expressed her disappointment that I decided not to return to school.

One of the best decisions that my mom ever made was sending me to a local college. I produced excellent grades in the first and second quarters, and I could have stayed on track for graduation. But I was not ready for college; I continued to battle the internal demons that were created as a result of my childhood trauma. I didn't know how to articulate to my mom how the anger, hurt, distress, and abandonment affected my mental state.

I wasn't so grown up after all. After I dropped out of college, I drifted through a series of meaningless jobs trying to figure out what I wanted to do next. I worked at a convenience store, a one-hour photo processing center, a grocery store, and in a clerical role for the City of Fontana. I was going nowhere fast.

To complicate matters even further, the relationship with the airman, which I had valued more than I had valued college, ended after I suffered a miscarriage.

This is Life

The key to success is to refuse to be basic;
you cannot be fulfilled living in the shadows of a dream
that you don't take the steps to realize.

CHAPTER THIRTEEN

Until Immaturity Do Us Part

*In the heart of every struggle
lies an opportunity to grow.*

~ Melanie M. Koulouris

O ne year after I dropped out of college, I found an entry-level position at a residential facility in Redlands, California, that assisted children with developmental disabilities. I enjoyed caring for individuals with special needs. My time at this job helped me to find my passion for working in human services programs.

My duties entailed direct patient care. I bathed, fed, and toileted the children who were assigned to my unit. Most of the children used sign language and body gestures to communicate and relied on the staff to transport them in wheelchairs or hospital beds.

With few exceptions, the children living there were wards of the State of California and had only sporadic contact with family members. On my days off, I paid special attention to the children without regular visitors. I spent time styling their hair, buying them cute outfits, or bringing them stuffed animals. During my tenure at this facility, I discovered that I would rather pursue a degree in psychology than in nursing.

One afternoon in the summer of 1983, my mom requested that I stop by the pharmacy at Norton Air Force Base to pick up her prescriptions. I approached the counter, and a tall, charismatic 22-year-old pharmacy technician named Airman Gregory Harris greeted me.

I noticed him as I walked through the lobby. His smile widened and seemed to light up the entire room. I observed that he carried himself with an obvious air of self-assurance. As I waited for the prescription to be filled, we visited, and I learned that he had grown up in Baltimore, Maryland.

Before I left the pharmacy with the prescription, we exchanged phone numbers and conversed about meeting later. I was single and dating at the time that I met Gregory. He told me that he had a long-term girlfriend at home but that he wanted to spend time with me. Most military guys had girlfriends back home, so his admission didn't faze me.

I liked Gregory also, and I wanted to know more about him. The next weekend we met for our first date. We seemed compatible. The more time we spent together, the more I fell in love with him and his personality.

At this point I continued to try to figure out the plans for my life. Gregory had specific goals and knew what he wanted to accomplish in his military career. I found his self-reliant and secure demeanor attractive.

Over the next six months we became a couple, and the relationship progressed quickly. Against both sets of our parents' and many of our friends' advice, we moved into an apartment together in San Bernardino, approximately a twenty-minute drive from my mom's house and both of our jobs. I was ecstatic to be on my own and to build a future with Gregory. I hoped that our relationship would lead to marriage.

We maintained the apartment for ten months. Neither of us managed our money well, and the unpaid bills piled up. Prior to the end of the first year of the lease, we were evicted. A week before our scheduled move-out date, some random thugs broke into the apartment and stole every single piece of our rented furniture, even the refrigerator and the microwave. Lucky for us, the rental fees included insurance, and the replacement costs for the entirety of the household items were covered.

After we were evicted from our apartment, Gregory obtained approval to return to the barracks to live, and my mom welcomed me home. We continued to date, and in March of 1984, two weeks before my twentieth birthday, we were married.

We couldn't afford to have a wedding. With our marriage license in hand, we started the drive to Las Vegas, Nevada, to elope. Midway through the trip we decided to stop and exchange vows at a chapel in Victorville, California. Neither of us had money for wedding rings. We planned to purchase them once our finances stabilized. We decided that we wanted to save money before leasing our next apartment, so my mom agreed to allow us to move into my old bedroom. She liked Gregory, and they had a cordial relationship.

As Gregory and I settled into our roles as husband and wife, we discovered that we both had a lot to learn about marriage. Gregory's personality was authoritative, and I also had a strong temperament. Neither of us communicated well, and we faced ups and downs during the early stages of our marriage.

Our disagreements often originated from power struggles because we both wanted to gain a sense of control. I was barely 20 years old and learning to navigate a lifelong commitment was harder to achieve after my enchanted images of marriage dissolved.

Four months after we tied the knot, Gregory received orders to transfer to Lackland Air Force Base in San Antonio, Texas, where we moved into base housing. Gregory served as a drill sergeant for the 3723 Basic Military Training Squadron, where new recruits were monitored on a twenty-four-hour basis.

Gregory worked with male recruits twelve to sixteen hours per day, and he valued the opportunity to shape the lives of the young men who joined the air force to serve their country.

Within the first month, I secured a job in a group home for adults with disabilities. I also enjoyed my job and signed up for overtime hours due to staffing shortages. My regular shift was 12:00 a.m. to 8:00 a.m. The extra hours that I worked varied between the morning and afternoon shifts.

Most of the time it seemed as though Gregory and I passed each other on our way to and from work. The more that we worked, the less time we spent together. The less time we spent together, the more I longed for the attention and the closeness that we had when we first met.

On one hand, I understood the demands and stressors of his job, but as a 20-year-old young lady, I wanted to go out to dinner and to the nightclubs to dance and to listen to music. I accepted two to three over-time shifts per week, and we made enough money to afford to go out on occasion.

I associated with some of my co-workers and one of the wives who lived on base. On my days off I spent time away from home with them, and we went dancing and attended events together. At the time I focused on my need to have fun, not the needs of my husband and not the needs of us as a couple. It soon became obvious that my approach was wrong. Gregory and I argued constantly, and we drifted apart. The intimate connection that we had once enjoyed in our relationship faded.

I was married, but I was lonely. I lacked the strength and maturity to realize that marriage takes sacrifice. I regret that I did not understand how to articulate my desires and acknowledge that Gregory also deserved time to learn how to be a husband.

In early 1986 during a visit with my dad in North Carolina, he and I spoke about my marriage. He advised me that I needed to decide if I wanted to be married or single. When he stated that I '*needed to do better and be better*' these words resonated in my head. He never said *I told you so*, but I knew him well enough to decipher what he meant, that I was too young for marriage.

Throughout my stay with my dad, I had a headache and vomited every day. I denied that I could be pregnant. The thought of bringing a baby into a marriage built on a wobbly foundation terrified me.

When I returned home to San Antonio, I went to the doctor, and he confirmed that I was twelve weeks pregnant. My emotions gyrated between elation and fear.

Gregory and I had not intended to have a baby so early in our relationship. I was 21 years old and pregnant for the third time, but I considered this baby a blessing. My preparations shifted into overdrive. I converted a guest room into a nursery, and I purchased so many baby items that I filled all the available space in the closet. I hoped that our child would solidify the bedrock of our marriage.

I communicated with both my mom and my dad weekly during my pregnancy. They both conveyed excitement about the baby, and we all prayed for the birth of a girl.

During my second trimester, my dad's COPD and CHF diagnosis resulted in repeated admissions to the hospital. His illness had progressed to the point that he needed oxygen around the clock. His health worsened as each day passed.

The thought of losing my dad caused me anxiety. I couldn't fathom living without him. During my second trimester, my sister Gwen notified Gregory and I that we needed to fly to North Carolina as soon as possible. The doctors projected that my dad would not live through the weekend.

The day after she called, Gregory and I arrived at the Albert Ellis Airport in Jacksonville shortly before midnight and headed straight to the were over when we arrived, but we appealed to the members of the nursing staff to grant us permission to see my dad.

As expected, my mom had flown in from California, and when I walked into the hospital room she sat at his bedside.

My dad anticipated my arrival. "I knew that you would come."

"Of course, I would be here for you. You are the first man I ever loved."

His pasty face indicated that he would transition to heaven at any time. He rubbed my protruding belly, and I rested my head on his chest until the nurse shooed all of us out of the room so he could rest. Seventy-two hours later my dad passed. The words he spoke to me during my last visit at home with him, *"I need to do better and be better"*, formed a text cloud above my head that haunted me in my dreams.

I gave birth to my beautiful daughter, Chantell Chavonn Harris, on November 11, 1986, five months after his death. I regretted that my dad's death preceded her entry into the world.

Her birth blessed our lives. However, the problems in our marriage increased after she was born. In April of 1987 I decided to return to North Carolina and give both Gregory and me a break to decide if we wanted to commit to making the marriage work. I resisted leaving. I wanted my daughter to grow up in a two-parent household. I also wanted to provide Chantell with the security that I had lacked as a child.

CHAPTER FOURTEEN

It's Time to Get it Together, Sister

> *They always say that time changes things,*
> *but you actually have to change them*
> *yourself.*
>
> ~ Andy Warhol

After my dad's death my mom returned to Jacksonville to live in the family home and spend time with her children and grandchildren. Upon my arrival from Texas in April of 1987, I planned to stay at the house with her for three months to find a job, save for an apartment, and enroll in school. Within a month, I changed my mind and decided to find an apartment for Chantell and me post haste. I enjoyed having my mom nearby, but I knew that after living on my own I could not adapt to a new set of household rules.

I found a two-bedroom, seven hundred-square-foot apartment in the New River area of Jacksonville. I signed a six-month lease and moved in with two suitcases full of clothes, one for Chantell and one for me, and some household items that my sisters Gwen and Joyce and my mom gave me. With money from my savings account, I purchased living room furniture, a bedroom set, and a television. Chantell and I slept together in a bed, and I began the process of rebuilding my life. I didn't know if Gregory and I would reconcile, so I needed to prepare myself for independence.

I applied for a position with the Onslow County government to work as a behavioral health technician for a detoxification center. I interviewed for the job, and the nursing director hired me based on my experience working in the children's residential facility in California.

I completed the admission process for individuals who came to the facility to cleanse their system of alcohol and drugs. At times the clients sought treatment on their own, but others were sent to the center by law enforcement after being arrested for public intoxication.

Thanks to the help of financial aid, I could afford to take classes at Coastal Carolina Community College. I worked the overnight shift, which ended at 7:00 a.m., and then headed to an 8:00 class. My last class ended at noon. Working the overnight shift and going straight to school fatigued me, but I focused on my goal of earning a degree and saving money.

Transportation was an issue without a car, but I managed. The detoxification center was less than a mile from the college. On some days a co-worker dropped me off on campus, and some days I walked. After two years of working for the county, I accepted a position for an organization that operated a group home for boys who were ordered into treatment for behavioral health issues by a juvenile court judge.

After a failed attempt at a reunion, my divorce from Gregory was finalized in 1988. Without the extra money that he sent to me on occasion, the four-thousand-dollar annual raise at the new job would allow me to meet my financial obligations. My mom gifted me with five hundred dollars to purchase a used car.

Six months into the job the director of the facility made sexual advances toward me. I was completely caught off guard by his behavior. I knew that he had a wife and children at home and his advances were very off-putting. He understood my situation as a single parent and knowing that I needed my job I believe that he attempted to exploit my vulnerabilities. I needed the money, so I tolerated his behavior for a time.

The director was an unethical person who also stole from the company. I reported the director's actions to the regional manager in hopes of having him removed from his job, but my idea backfired. I was unaware that my boss and the regional manager were friends. As a result, the director terminated my employment without notice. If I had been more astute at the time, I would have filed a sexual harassment lawsuit and fought for my rights.

One month prior to losing my job I purchased a brand-new Toyota Tercel and moved from the apartment in New River to a three-bedroom rental house so that Chantell would have a safe place to play. I had a thousand dollars in the bank, but I was unprepared to be off work without earning a paycheck for any length of time.

During the two months that it took me to find another position, I survived on my savings, a loan from my mother, $275.00 per month in child support, and $250.00 per month in food stamps.

Applying for food stamps awakened a fire inside of me. I never expected to be in a government office applying for public assistance. But I knew that my situation was temporary, and I often thought about my dad's words that I could *do better.*

I found a minimum wage position at a private residential facility for adults with disabilities in Swansboro, located twenty miles from Jacksonville. Since I had a car, I didn't worry about transportation. I barely paid my bills on time with my salary, but the money was better than sitting at home without income. Although I knew that my mom would continue to help me if I asked, I wanted to manage my responsibilities and support my daughter on my own. I never lost my drive and motivation to obtain my degree and embark upon a successful career.

At my new job, much of the staff had served the organization for three to five years. I was an outsider, and staff members rebuffed my input. Frequent conflicts occurred between the various employee cliques. I refused to be consumed by the stress and dedicated my energy to caring for the residents.

One day I arrived fifteen minutes early for my shift, and my supervisor summoned me to her office. She handed me a termination notice and informed me that my co-workers had complained about my work. Although my supervisor never gave me any feedback of a critical nature or any written documentation that indicated poor performance, I lost my job.

When the supervisor failed to provide me with any specifics about my work, I gathered my belongings and left the building. To this day I am unable to pinpoint a valid reason that I was let go except that God knew that I needed to leave Jacksonville, North Carolina, to further my education.

CHAPTER FIFTEEN

Eagle Pride

*Education is the most powerful weapon
that you can use to change the world.*

~ Nelson Mandela

Sometimes we must pay attention to the signs that are sent our way, even when they appear at the most inopportune time. After two terminations in one year, I declined to wait around for a third message. I knew that I had to make some changes.

Meaningful employment prospects without a college degree were limited in Jacksonville. If I chose to remain in the area, I would be relegated to entry-level positions commensurate with my background at group homes or skilled nursing facilities.

In the summer of 1990, I decided that I needed to move to Durham, North Carolina, a city within proximity to universities with bachelor's and master's-level programs.

But I faced a dilemma. I didn't know one single person in Durham. I had a 4-year-old daughter at home and the drive between Jacksonville and Durham was two and a half hours. I needed to work and go to school, and I didn't want Chantell to spend twelve to sixteen hours a day with a babysitter. I was thankful that my sister Gwen and my mom volunteered to keep Chantell at the family home in Jacksonville.

The decision to leave Chantell with Gwen and my mom troubled me because I could not see her each day. As parents we often try to give our children what we did not have but needed from our own parents. As a child I needed to believe that my mom did not abandon me. But, I always held the thought in the back of my mind that she did.

For this reason, I wanted Chantell to understand that I was not abandoning her and that I was not away from her so that I could be free and have fun. I had a lot on my plate, but I never wanted Chantell to worry that I wouldn't bring her to Durham when I graduated from college.

Before I began school, I needed to find a job and an apartment. I planned to work for one-year and pay off my outstanding bills before submitting any applications to college. Prior to relocating to Durham, I applied for work with fifteen organizations, and I fielded several offers of employment. I settled on a company in whose employ I remained during my entire time in Durham, P.C. Contract Management. Upon being hired, I worked as a paraprofessional in direct care and earned a promotion to group home manager six months later.

I visited the campus of North Carolina Central University in January of 1991. Even as a 26-year-old, I could hardly contain my glee when I toured the buildings and learned about the rich history of the school. The professors in the psychology department answered my questions and discussed the components of the curriculum with me. Each of the student guides expressed the reasons they chose to attend NCCU. I purchased a t-shirt with the slogan *"Eagle Pride Amplified"* emblazoned across the front.

My acceptance letter to NCCU arrived in the mail in May of 1991. With the credits that I had earned at San Bernardino Valley College and Coastal Carolina Community College, I was classified as a junior.

In the summer of 1991, I took introduction to abnormal psychology for my first class. I was comfortable on campus and felt a sense of belonging that is hard to describe. The positive energy in the atmosphere and the sense of connectedness between the students inspired me.

I have always performed well under pressure. I worked fifty to sixty hours a week and carried a full-time school load. I spent many late nights studying and writing papers. I wanted to graduate with honors. On the occasions when keeping numerous balls in the air became hectic, I imagined myself walking across the stage in my cap and gown with an honor cord draped around my neck.

Some mornings I rose at 4:00 a.m. to drive to Jacksonville to have breakfast or lunch with Chantell for special events at school and then drove back to Durham on the same day. I adjusted my work schedule to be present for all birthdays and holidays.

When graduation rolled around in 1993, I floated on air. I completed my degree according to my timeline and graduated with Cum Laude honors. My mom followed me around the house all morning snapping pictures with a huge smile on her face. She had waited eleven years for me to finish college. I made her happy that day, and her presence for one of the most significant events in my life was gratifying to me.

Although I am the only one of my siblings to earn a four-year degree, my sisters Gwen and Joyce pulled for me harder than I pulled for myself at times. They encouraged me, gave me financial support when needed, and prayed for me.

I will always be grateful for their help and constant support. When they cared for Chantell for me, I didn't worry about finding babysitters or missing school or work. Without the support of my family during this time, I am not sure that I would have achieved my current level of success.

It was a priceless moment to have Chantell there at my graduation. She has attended the ceremonies for each degree that I have earned, from my bachelor's degree to my doctorate.

Attending North Carolina Central University changed my life and served a major role in my educational success. The mascot for the school is an Eagle, which symbolizes strength, courage, wisdom, and healing, each of the elements of my life that I pursued during my time there. I am pleased to call myself an Eagle, and on my graduation day my *pride was indeed amplified.*

CHAPTER SIXTEEN

A New Phase Begins

> *The beginning*
> *is always today.*
>
> ~ Mary Shelley

Once I graduated from NCCU, I brought Chantell to live with me in Durham. I enrolled her in a summer program at the Salvation Army Boys and Girls Club during the day.

As soon as I completed my degree, my director promoted me to the position of regional administrator/clinical supervisor managing four residential facilities for adults with intellectual disabilities.

Each day I drove two hours or more round-trip to Lee-Harnett County where the facilities were located. I managed my schedule so that I could pick Chantell up before the Boys and Girls club closed for the evening. On occasion when I needed to work overtime, my friends Nancy or Annie stepped in and cared for Chantell until I arrived home.

For the first time in my life, I viewed myself as a complete, self-reliant person. I decided to apply to graduate school at NCCU to study clinical psychology. I began the program in the fall of 1993 when Chantell started the first grade. Each day I juggled a routine that consisted of helping her with homework, after-school activities, commuting, taking evening classes, and writing papers.

I hired an undergraduate student as a nanny. She picked Chantell up from the Boys and Girls Club two days a week, brought her home, and got her settled and ready for bed. On occasion, Chantell attended classes with me when the nanny was unavailable.

In 1994, my mom found a large lump in her armpit and made an appointment with her physician. One week later, he gave her a diagnosis of breast cancer. The news devastated my siblings and me. We supported her through the process of undergoing chemotherapy and a mastectomy.

After her treatment concluded, her cancer went into remission, and she resumed working and all of her regular activities. My sisters and I increased the time that we spent with my mom. I typically drove to Jacksonville almost every weekend. Although my siblings and I were all grown and living our own lives, we still tried to re-capture the time we missed with her when she left the house twenty-three years before.

CHAPTER SEVENTEEN

Life Transitions

> *Sometimes, the most interesting things*
> *may be found when you are not*
> *looking for anything.*
>
> ~ Anonymous

When I met my friend Annie in 1991, she became my confidant and I considered her to be an adopted member of my family. She accompanied me on many of my trips to Jacksonville, and we liked dancing at the local clubs.

One early morning in January of 1995 we decided to go to a diner for breakfast. As we chatted and laughed as usual, we noticed two handsome guys sitting at a table behind us, who kept looking our way.

We tried to act oblivious and continued to enjoy our meal. Thirty minutes later as we paid our bill and headed towards the door to leave the restaurant, the two guys approached us.

One of the young men held the door open as we exited and said, "well, hello lovely ladies, you two sure are looking pretty, what's your name?"

Annie and I exchanged a quick glance between each other. Sometimes we used pseudonyms when we met guys in Jacksonville, especially if they greeted us rudely or we felt a bad vibe when they spoke to us. This time, however, I gladly introduced myself and offered Annie's name before she had a chance to speak.

"So nice to meet you, I am Alvin, and this guy over here is my best friend Kea". He grabbed my hand and I noticed that he wore a gold necklace with an eagle, a globe, and an anchor on it, the emblem of the United States Marine Corps.

"So, you are in the Marine Corps?" I asked.

"Yes," he beamed as he stepped closer to me. "How did you know?"

"I recognize the symbol on your necklace. My dad served in the Marine Corps." His chest seemed to swell as I imagined he was pleased to learn that we might have something in common.

We spoke briefly, and I took his number, promising to call him later in the week. Once I returned home and resumed my schedule, I was again swamped with managing the daily tasks of being a single mom, a student, and a full-time manager with a long commute, so I never made the phone call. As time passed, I forgot about my promise to call Alvin and misplaced the number.

Nine months later, in the autumn of 1995, Chantell and I were in Jacksonville heading to the Marine Corps Exchange at the New River Air Station, and a car pulled up alongside us at the stoplight.

The driver and I traded glances, and then I realized that it was Alvin. He also recognized me. He followed my car to the Exchange and we conversed for a few minutes before swapping numbers. Over the next week we spoke on the phone almost daily.

At the time that we reconnected I had recently ended a relationship, and he had been separated from his wife for more than a year and she lived in a different state. Alvin was the father of two girls, Kiara, age 4, and Ariana, age 3. Through talking, we recognized that we both loved seafood, southern cooking, and music.

We started dating and I wanted to take things slow so that we could both be sure that our current relationships were over. When we met, I had been divorced for nearly eight years, and I had no desire to become involved in a complicated fling.

Three months after our chance encounter, my mom learned that her cancer had returned and metastasized to her liver. She underwent chemotherapy again and dealt with debilitating side effects, such as a low blood count, alopecia, and extreme weight loss. During her course of treatment, she often developed infections that resulted in her admission to Lenoir Memorial Hospital in Kinston, North Carolina, a one-hour drive from Jacksonville and a three-hour drive from Durham.

Though my coursework was completed and I was in the process of writing my thesis, I put graduate school on hold. I needed to focus on my mom's health. During her stays at the hospital in Kinston, I drove from Durham to see her for one or two hours each day. Her immune system was compromised during chemotherapy, so Chantell was limited to standing outside the door of her hospital room and waving to her from afar.

When my mom's cancer recurred, I was grief-stricken. Most of the time I didn't know if I was coming or going, so I leaned on Alvin for strength.

Annie stayed at my house in Durham to watch Chantell, and I took time off work to stay at my mom's bedside during the day. My sister, Gwen monitored her health at night. Alvin arranged to take military leave to accompany me when I took my mom to chemotherapy, driving us back and forth from Jacksonville to the appointments in Kinston.

Each day I saw my mom withering away before my eyes. She continued to lose weight and grew weaker. Even still, when the doctor informed us that the chemotherapy regimen had failed and she had less than three months to live, the news shattered my family.

In the first week of January in 1996, we decided to place my mom in palliative care services at home. The doctors prescribed morphine to keep her comfortable and she was able to communicate with us through written notes and gestures. By the end of the second week her cognitive abilities declined, and she floated in and out of consciousness. On the morning of January 12th, I noticed that she was unresponsive to verbal cues; so Alvin and I decided to make an appointment with her physician in Kinston to have her evaluated.

Alvin carried her to the car, placed her in the back seat, and we drove her to the doctor's office. The doctor admitted her to the hospital, and Alvin and I spent the night sleeping next to her bedside in an uncomfortable recliner.

Two days after her admission to the hospital she succumbed to cancer. I grieved internally and externally shifted to fix-it mode.

My siblings leaned on me to handle the arrangements. I organized the funeral services, fielded phone calls, managed the finances, wrote the obituary, and served as superwoman by day. At night, I lost my composure and cried myself to sleep in Alvin's arms.

After my mom passed, I took three months off work, taking advantage of the Family Medical Leave Act. I experienced bouts of depression and had a difficult time concentrating on the activities I normally enjoyed. Losing my mother induced a flood of latent, unsettled emotions that seemed to hit me all at once.

During the same period, I wanted Alvin to decide about his divorce and the status of our relationship. He conveyed his ambivalence about proceeding with the dissolution of his marriage. I understood the sentiments he expressed, and I admired the love and devotion he had to Kiara and Ariana.

Alvin supported me throughout the ordeal of my mom's death, one of the worst moments of my life. However, I was unwilling to continue to invest my time in a relationship with an uncertain future.

Four months after my mom's death Alvin and I parted ways so that both of us could have the space to determine our next steps. His divorce filing was complete, but we needed the distance and time alone. We stayed in communication and remained on favorable terms.

In October of 1996, Alvin was selected for an elite position as a recruiter assigned to the Marine Corps Recruiting Station in Dallas, Texas. The geographical distance between us magnified the feelings of affection that I held for him. I also realized that taking a break from the relationship enhanced our friendship. In January of 1997, I began flying to Dallas monthly; we toured the different areas of the city and affirmed that we wanted to reunite as a couple. After a multitude of discussions, we were married in May of 1997.

*Time will pass
every single day no matter what,
so why not maximize your desire
to live your best life?*

CHAPTER EIGHTEEN

The Not-So-Great State of Texas

New beginnings bring new possibilities,
a chance to this time get it right.

~ Lynn M. McHale

By June of 1997, I resided in the State of Texas for the second time in my life. Alvin and I rented a four-bedroom home in the city of Richardson in a picturesque, quiet neighborhood. The home was within walking distance of the school that Chantell attended and Alvin's office.

After six weeks of searching, I secured a job in Flower Mound, an hour drive from Richardson. Traveling outside of my home community for work was common for me. However, I could not tolerate the daily commute and the traffic jams that extended my time on the interstate. Although I liked the company I worked for, I soon sought a position closer to home.

In September of 1997, I accepted an offer of employment to serve as the director of the home and community-based services program (HCS) for Dallas County Mental Health and Mental Retardation Services. I managed thirty residential facilities and two hundred employees.

The previous director had resigned, and I inherited a program plagued by deficiencies, high turnover rates, client abuse, cost overruns, and employees who resisted my charge to make wide-scale changes.

As a requirement to operate HCS programs that were funded by the State of Texas, providers are required to undergo an annual survey to ensure that the policies were implemented according to the prescribed guidelines. Throughout the five-year history of HCS, multiple citations were levied in areas ranging from medication errors to failure to follow the client's treatment plans. Instead of the customary annual visits, reviewers from the state visited the program on a quarterly basis to assess the implementation of the plan of correction.

The chief executive officer committed to providing the resources and support that I needed to overhaul the program. After a year of re-organizing the staffing structure and developing a strategic framework, in January of 1999, the department passed the annual survey with one deficiency related to a missing consent form.

After the fifth year of inception, the State of Texas finally deemed the HCS program to be in compliance. The success came at a cost.

From September through November of 1998, my team worked twelve-hour shifts four days a week to prepare for the survey. This meant that at times Chantell spent the evening with my neighbor and her children, other times she stayed home alone.

Chantell was 12 years old by that time, and I regret the moments I spent away from her in pursuit of my career aspirations. I liked claiming triumph for developing new standards for the program and hearing the countless accolades from the state officials but losing time with my daughter was not worth attaining any of my goals.

Alvin began his role as a recruiter as an E-6 Staff Sergeant with eleven years of service. In the Marine Corps, the roles of recruiter and drill instructor were widely viewed as two of the most difficult positions.

The selection process for both specialty billets includes an evaluation of the Marine's qualifications by a screening team that is assigned to Headquarters Marine Corps in Quantico, Virginia. Each candidate submits a file with copies of their service commendations, training records, and performance reviews for assessment. To be selected for a recruiter or a drill instructor post, the Marine must be ranked within the higher echelon of their peers.

On the surface, the tasks for a recruiter may appear simple. However, Alvin had a quota of recruiting three qualified men or women each month. If the goal was unmet, the month was considered a failure.

A qualified recruit is considered an individual who has earned a high school diploma, passed the Armed Services Vocational Aptitude Battery, cleared a background check, met physical fitness standards, and provided proof of legal residency in the United States.

The pool of prospects regarded as eligible to serve as Marines could vary based on the assigned geographic area of the recruiter, the economy, and the state of the nation. Alvin's area of assignment covered a well-established community where the parents had high income levels and the majority of students he interviewed planned to attend college.

To add to the complexity of meeting the monthly quota, an applicant could not be classified as a recruit until each of the conditions were met. This meant that a potential recruit might not be 'counted' as a success for three to six months after the initial meeting. On rare occasions, the provisions could be completed within 30 days. Once the prerequisites were met, the recruits were required to complete the basic training process.

To compound the difficulty of recruiting interested prospects, the basic training for Marine Corps recruits extends over a thirteen-week period compared to eight weeks of training for the Air Force and ten weeks of training for the Navy and the Army.

Alvin worked twelve hour shifts Monday through Saturday, a schedule that is typical for recruiters. The amount of quality time that we spent together as a family was limited. Although Alvin seldom communicated his concerns about his work, I knew that the job was mentally taxing. He focused on meeting the monthly quota to solidify his chances for a future promotion.

Enlisted Marines are limited to serving for a maximum of thirty years. Alvin had high expectations of reaching the terminal rank of E-9, a master gunnery sergeant, before his mandatory retirement. Attaining the quota throughout the duration of his assignment could elevate his chances with a promotion review board.

When his monthly quota was met and I was not spinning in circles because of work, we got along well. When he didn't achieve the quota, our communication decreased, our sense of connectedness ebbed, and a chasm grew between us.

In the nine years before our marriage, I had grown accustomed to independently managing my household and living alone. Likewise, Alvin routinely assumed the obligation for taking care of many of the members of his extended family.

We were both strong-willed. Neither one of us knew how to loosen the invisible reins to which we each held so tightly. It has been said that the first year of marriage is tough but describing our first year of marriage as such would be an understatement.

We lived on a seesaw of periods of stability and bouts of conflict. We co-existed in a continuous cycle of being on the verge of separation.

Just as I did, I am sure that he contemplated running away from home on a regular basis. Through my observations of the problems between other recruiters and their spouses, I knew that our situation was not unique.

I longed to have a baby, but I knew that the timing was not right given the fragility of our relationship, the demands of both of our jobs, and the financial stress of paying over a thousand dollars a month for childcare expenses.

Alvin paid a substantial amount of money in child support, and I dedicated my extra funds to paying off my credit card debt so that I could return to school. I hoped that my dream of having a son would be realized at some time in the future.

Once again, I lived in Texas, married to a military man with a difficult job, and I questioned the security of my marriage. I convinced myself that I was jinxed by the state, and I wanted to leave Texas as soon as possible.

Lift your feet off the ground today
and reach as high as you can.
No one ever achieves their goals
by keeping their feet firmly planted
safely to the ground.

CHAPTER NINETEEN

I'm Going Back to Cali

> *It is said that time heals all wounds,*
> *but how am I going to get through*
> *today?*
>
> ~ Dr. Marie Brown Mercadel

In February of 2000, Alvin received orders transferring him to the Marine Corps Air Station Miramar in San Diego, California. I highly anticipated a move to a location where he could work fewer hours, be freed from a monthly quota, and spend more time with our family.

I also knew that the career opportunities in California were vast. I actively researched open positions within the city and county government system, places to live, and the best-rated schools.

For me, Alvin's transfer orders could not have come at a better time. I was elated and ready to leave Texas. I had grown tired of my job, his work hours, and the aura of bad karma and negative energy that I sensed in my surroundings.

Three months after the orders were issued, my euphoria turned to heartbreak. Alvin broke the news to me that he had an affair with a girl in Dallas and that she had given birth to a baby. I didn't know which was worse, the ache in my heart, his betrayal, my desire to cause bodily harm to him, or the fact that we didn't have a child together. I would have never expected to learn that he fathered a child while engaged in a clandestine liaison.

So many random thoughts penetrated my mind, and those old childhood insecurities rose to the surface once again. The questions were numerous. *How did this happen? Why did this happen? Should I leave? Can I ever trust him again? Who is this person to whom I am married? Did I make a mistake marrying him and leaving North Carolina?*

When Alvin told me about the baby in April of 2000, he had already transferred to California, and I remained in Texas so that Chantell could finish the school year. I pondered staying in Texas, moving back to North Carolina, or hightailing it to anywhere else in the world. I consulted with an attorney, who completed the divorce paperwork. We didn't have joint marital assets, credit card bills, or money to fight over. However, I couldn't bring myself to sign the forms.

For days I refused to accept his telephone calls. When I finally answered I listened to his apologies and assurances that the affair and the girl with whom he had had the affair *didn't mean anything* to him and a host of other explanations about why we should stay together. My rage and disappointment increased each time I thought about picking up my entire life and moving to Texas when we got married.

I would never wish my desolation and despair on another person, be it a friend or an enemy. I held Alvin responsible for my agony. The fact that he had an affair had an adverse impact on our marriage and my trust level for him dropped to zero.

In my present frame of thought, I knew that I did not possess the emotional bandwidth to act as a stepmom to a baby born as the result of Alvin's affair. The baby was an innocent casualty in the messy dynamic. However, the toll of the affair rendered me unable to assume a role that I hadn't signed up for.

I refused to assume the burden of creating a resolution for a situation that I did not create. I set boundaries for the way that I would handle the issue, and Alvin needed to make his decisions by taking those boundaries into consideration.

I understood that he wanted to have a relationship with his new daughter, and I didn't interfere with his desire to do so. I expected there to be communication between he and the girl with whom he had had the affair for the sake of the baby. I left him to cope with the tribulations that accompanied the consequences of his actions.

My fury and resentment sat on my back like a ton of bricks. I was smart, educated, attractive, and independent, yet somehow, I tolerated a scenario that had resulted in immediate divorces for thousands of couples.

An ancient axiom is that time heals all wounds. I have yet to find a sensible explanation about what to do when time moves at the speed of an injured turtle.

To make matters worse, my internal insecurities prevented me from confiding in my sisters about the baby. They were experts at cutting people off, and I knew that they would shun Alvin. I dealt with the sorrow alone in my own head.

The thought of confiding in my friends about the affair produced waves of humiliation. It is difficult to compartmentalize the different components of one's life. But I managed to lock away the sting of the affair in a box of discarded sentiments.

I proceeded with living my life and made sure that Chantell adjusted well to two major moves in three years. Time would tell if the marriage would survive. I didn't have the time or patience to wallow in misery. I needed to live my life and push ahead with my goals.

Don't let negativity define you or destroy you,

your dreams, or your aspirations.

CHAPTER TWENTY

Moving Forward Standing Still

> *Smile,*
> *even when it hurts.*
>
> ~ Unknown

I moved to San Diego in June of 2000. I have never heard a person complain about residing in San Diego. Surrounded by pristine beaches, 70-degree weather on most days, and a diverse population of people, it would be difficult to find a reason to criticize living there.

Prior to my arrival in San Diego, I secured a job with the County Health and Human Services Agency working as the executive assistant to the director of aging and adult services. The employees in the division provided a variety of services for older adults and people with disabilities.

I attended community meetings, developed the departmental business plan, revised policies, assisted with writing board letters, and a few other duties. The position required direct interface with members of the community, advocacy groups, and state and local partners.

I assumed the lead role of managing the implementation of the Gallup Organization's concept of engagement, a governance model that focuses on the culture of the workplace and its effect on employee satisfaction and productivity. These duties changed my entire outlook on the meaning of job satisfaction and work environments in which people thrive.

I learned that the culture of an organization is more important than the precise execution of any strategic blueprint. My new boss taught me how to focus on employee strengths, as opposed to attempting to fix their *weaknesses*. I threw out the adage of treating every employee the same, and instead I learned to treat employees according to their individual assets.

Studying the Gallup framework gave me insight into my personal strengths and influenced my thought process about my obligations as a leader. Later in my career I became a certified Gallup coach and trained frontline supervisors and managers how to understand the needs of their staff.

Fueled by my work with Gallup, in August of 2000 I enrolled at the University of Phoenix to pursue a master's degree in organizational leadership. I attended classes at a satellite location in San Diego and participated in a study group for a total of eight hours a week. Fortunately, my employer did not have an expectation for me to work extended hours. I managed my work and school schedule with ample time to support the activities in which Chantell participated as an eighth-grade, middle-school student.

Alvin supported my desire to attend school and he often cared for Chantell and attended her events if I needed extra time to complete assignments. Although his work responsibilities included the supervision of over three hundred Marines', he made the adjustments that were needed to spend more time at home with Chantell and I.

While studying for my master's degree, I wanted to learn about the research related to child abuse and neglect and the psychological and physiological impacts of trauma. To support my approach to healing, I needed to enhance my knowledge so that I could use any information that would help to guide my restorative process.

In 2002, I signed up to attend a conference to learn about the Kaiser Permanente and Centers for Disease Control and Prevention (CDC) Adverse Childhood Experiences Study (ACES, Appendix A), which was conducted in 1998. Adverse Childhood Experiences are described as traumatic events that occur between the ages of birth to 17 years. Seventeen thousand members of a health maintenance organization in California completed a confidential survey about their childhood experiences, health history, and social challenges in adulthood.

The participants responded to ten survey questions about common traumatic experiences that occur in early life before the age of 18. According to the findings of the study, the higher the score on the ACES survey, the higher the likelihood that a person will experience psychological issues related to behavioral health disorders in adulthood.

In addition, the Kaiser Permanente and CDC researchers indicated that individuals with an ACES score of four or more were prone to substance abuse, unwanted pregnancies, domestic violence, heart disease, obesity, and other detrimental experiences that could result in a shortened lifespan.

Additional findings implied that emotional issues such as depression, anxiety, and feelings of unworthiness might also affect individuals who suffered from childhood trauma.

I barely moved as I listened to the presenter, and at times I held my breath. As the questions flashed on the screen, I answered each one in my head: *no, no, yes, yes, no, yes, yes, no, yes, and no.*

My affirmative responses related to domestic violence, sexual abuse, divorce/separation, experiencing depression, and feeling unloved as a child. The key findings from the study indicated that one-third of the population reported the occurrence of adverse child experiences (CDC, 2021).

More than two-thirds of the population reported responding *yes* to three or more of the study questions and were at risk for experiencing toxic stress (Stork et al., 2020).

Learning about the study empowered me with new information that held implications for both my personal and professional life. Understanding the evidence-based exploration of childhood trauma did not provide an overnight cure for me. But accessing the resources that I needed laid the groundwork for me to acknowledge that I needed counseling.

Utilizing the tools necessary to thrive after trauma is different for everyone. To counter the effects of the sexual molestation I decided that I would join a therapy group, reveal the components of my life story to others, and use my voice to empower girls and boys to speak out about their own abuse. Before I could take any of those actions, I first needed to reflect on the plight of my marriage.

CHAPTER TWENTY-ONE

Life is a Gift, Living is a Blessing

> *Each person makes a choice about whether their life contributions will have a positive or a negative impact on society.*
>
> ~ Dr. Marie Brown Mercadel

The aftermath of the affair lingered. I knew that Alvin's inability to bring the child to our home to interact with Chantell, Kiara, and Ariana made him sad. He traveled to see her in Texas each year, but it would be eighteen years before I agreed to visits in our home. While part of me understood the dilemma he faced, I needed to protect my sanity and peace of mind.

I did my best to move toward recovering from Alvin's entanglement. I made genuine efforts in my marriage, but at the same time I continued to position myself for the possibility that I could be single again in the future. My reactions alternated between outrage at Alvin and compassion for the child.

I often reflected about whether my marriage would last. While some parts of my life thrived, such as school and work, another part of my life, my marriage, seemed to be held in suspense.

In some ways, Alvin's betrayal of my trust motivated me to complete school and focus on climbing the ladder of success.

I needed to prove to myself that I was enough.

As a novice human services professional, I did not make the connection between my early trauma as a child and my reaction to situations as an adult. My approach to coping with the hurt mirrored my reaction to my previous trauma and learned behavior of self-protection. Some may view this as unhealthy, and I am agreeable with that, but my form of self-preservation was effective for me. My learned behaviors taught me how to mask my angst and contributed to the way in which I handled traumatic events.

One thing that is certain in life, the sun will rise in the morning and it will set every night. Regardless of what a person is confronting, time will not stand still. Each person is faced with the choice to live or to exist. I have seen so many people wake up each day to an existence while ignoring the promise and beauty of life.

While navigating the state of my marriage, I made a conscious decision each day to gain mental strength with the goal of becoming stronger. To do this, I needed to release the hurt, self-doubt, and anxieties that I carried around in an invisible suitcase that was wrapped around my neck.

Part of this required making a choice: either I would stay married and forgive Alvin for his betrayal, or I would divorce him. I loved him and I decided to stay in my marriage. In the moment of my decision, I didn't make a commitment to stay forever. I didn't promise that my anger and disappointment had vanished. Nor did I guarantee that I wouldn't change my mind and leave at later date. Instead, I entered into an agreement with myself that I would take care of my mental well-being first, and then I would try to emotionally lessen the insidious effects of Alvin's indiscretion.

CHAPTER TWENTY-TWO

Let's Do This Together

> *Hearts rebuilt from hope*
> *resurrect dreams killed by hate.*
>
> ~ Aberjhani

My decision to stay in the marriage was one that I took seriously. In spite of the affair, we both believed that we had enough love for each other to re-kindle the light in our relationship that existed when we started dating in 1995. Neither of us had any illusions that the painful parts of our history together would disappear. Instead, we held the belief that we would take one day at a time to stay connected even on the days that seemed less than positive.

For any couple that maintains their marriage after infidelity, the absence of trust is likely to be a topic of discussion on a regular basis. Alvin and I knew that we would need to embrace the option of engaging in therapy with a professional counselor if real change and healing was going to happen for us. We participated in twelve marital counseling sessions. I don't think that I expected to discover a magical answer as to why he had had an affair. Rather, I needed to gain some insight as to why I stayed in the marriage.

Our therapy sessions were intense. Sometimes we shouted, at times, I cried, we both became defensive, and we even ended a couple of sessions early because our lines of communication broke down. At times, I walked away from therapy even more confused.

Some days we walked around the house in silence and I would become too angry to articulate why my mood suddenly changed.

Mid-way through our counseling sessions I think we both had an epiphany in recognizing that in our quest to have a happy marriage, we first had to knock down the walls around our hearts. I needed to let go of my learned behavior of dealing with my pain by internalizing my feelings. For Alvin, it was necessary for him to forego the *tough guy* persona and reflect on the gravity of his behavior.

The therapist also emphasized what I already understood. He reminded me *"restoring the faith that I had when we first got married was a long road that would be filled with detours and sharp curves. Looming around the curves would be anger, frustration, and the desire to give-up on the marriage"*.

I knew that I needed empathy from Alvin. I wanted him to express authentic remorse and I rejected the excuses about the stress of recruiting duty or the long work hours or any other explanations for the affair. At the same time, he wanted patience and forgiveness from me, with the latter being a request that would take two years to achieve. Nonetheless, we moved forward in our marriage and continued the painstaking work that would be necessary to heal.

All things considered, we still enjoyed each other's company and made long-term plans for our future. After three years of paying rent, in August of 2003 we decided to start the process of purchasing our first house in San Diego. When we moved into our newly built home in 2004, this represented a huge milestone for Alvin and me as we devoted our energy to bridging the gaps in our relationship and reconstructing our marriage.

One year after we moved, in June of 2005, Chantell graduated from high school and moved to North Carolina to attend college. Later that same year, Alvin received orders to deploy to the Middle East for seven months. The forced separation was a catalyst for improving our communication through long emails; cherished telephone calls, letters, and text messages. Upon his return home in March of 2006, our union was on the road to recovery.

*If your dreams and aspirations
don't cause your stomach to hurt,
then the dream is not big enough.*

CHAPTER TWENTY-THREE

Laissez Les Bons Temps Rouler

*Happiness doesn't have
just one address.*

~ Anonymous

In typical military fashion, Alvin received transfer orders to the Naval Air Station Joint Reserve Base in New Orleans, Louisiana, in January of 2008. It appears that as soon as the last of the finishing touches were done on our new home, the movers packed up our belongings, and we were off to a different location.

The housing market in California continued to fluctuate. We knew that it was likely that we would return to California, so we rented our home instead of putting it on the market. We built a house in Gonzales, Louisiana, a city seventy miles from New Orleans. We remained there for the three years that we resided in Louisiana.

Alvin grew up in New Orleans, and he looked forward to residing within driving distance of his extended family that lived in the city, especially my mother-in-law, Susie. Though he traveled extensively in his position leading a quality control inspection team, we spent some weekends with his family and attended events such as birthday parties, graduations, Mardi Gras, the Jazz Festival, and the Essence Festival together. We also enjoyed hosting family functions at our home and frequently held gatherings for his friends and co-workers.

The State of Louisiana is divided into sixty-four parishes, the equivalent to counties in other states. I applied for positions in parishes that were within fifty miles of our home. In August of 2008, the Secretary of the Department of Children and Family Services in Baton Rouge Parish appointed me to serve as her confidential assistant.

The department provided statewide social services for children and families such as processing applications for public assistance programs, collecting child support, conducting child abuse investigations, and facilitating adoptions. The department also held the obligation to coordinate the sheltering and care for Louisiana citizens in the event of a natural disaster.

Barely two weeks into my role, Hurricane Gustav ravaged the state with winds of more than one hundred and ten miles per hour and was classified as the second major hurricane of the season. The secretary assigned me to work in the emergency operations center securing shelter placements for evacuees, attending daily briefings, and assisting with logistics, such as coordinating the delivery of food and medical supplies for displaced families.

I learned fast that the political environment in Louisiana government differed from my previous exposure to working with city and county officials in California and North Carolina. For reasons that I did not fully understand, the governor terminated my boss within four weeks of my appointment.

Newly installed by the governor, the interim secretary approached her role in an exacting manner with rigorous standards for performance. Our management philosophies were often in conflict, but we formed a collegial rapport, and in 2009 she selected me to serve on her executive team as the chief of staff.

One highlight of my role was to develop the protocols for the legislative process. This encompassed partnering with the legal and policy staff to draft bills, identifying a bill sponsor in the house or the senate, educating the members of the legislature, and ensuring that the governor signed the department-sponsored bills into law. The environment at work was partisan, fast-paced, and at times, destructive.

The demands of the job were constant, and I often worked more than sixty hours a week. On any given day, a crisis arose that resulted in the executive team working late into the evening to present a solution to the governor or members of his staff. We fielded text messages and telephone calls late at night and on the weekends.

I honed my analytical thinking skills, and my knowledge of working in state government grew. However, the long hours and constant shifting of priorities took a toll on me. The time had come for me to search for another job.

In May of 2010, as I sat in my car in my reserved parking space in the State of Louisiana parking garage gathering the mental resolve to begin another day of work, a former colleague who had previously worked in the governor's office called me. She had left her position to run for parish president of St. John the Baptist Parish, a position equivalent to the mayor of a city. She won the election and asked if I had an interest in serving as her chief administrative officer.

I had never given any thought to serving in a job outside of human services. Though the call could not have come at a better time, the request came as a total surprise. I accepted the job with all due zeal.

After the swearing-in ceremony, we went to work revising policies and procedures, re-defining standards for the contracting and bidding process, training staff, and developing a strategic plan.

I provided oversight to the directors of economic development, purchasing and contracting, health and human services, public works, sewer and water, recreation, public safety, and finance. I lacked expertise in managing municipal operations, but my education and proficiency serving in prior government entities equipped me for the position.

The constructs of leadership and management are the same across various industries. I trusted that if the directors possessed the skills to lead their teams, I could provide tactical direction and guidance.

My term in the position was short-lived. In May of 2011, Alvin received transfer orders to the Camp Pendleton Marine Corps Base in Oceanside, California, a community in the northern area of San Diego County. The movers packed up our belongings, we found a tenant for our house in Gonzales, and headed back to San Diego.

I will always be appreciative of the opportunity that I had to gain new experience and serve the residents of the St. John the Baptist Parish community.

CHAPTER TWENTY-FOUR

Duty Calls

Action and accountability
create opportunity

~ Garrison Wynn

As soon as I discovered that we would be returning to California, I contacted my former boss in San Diego County to inquire about the prospect of re-joining her team. The timing was critical. Within a month of my call a position became available, and the director of the health and human services agency selected me to serve as the assistant deputy director of regional operations.

In June of 2011, we returned to our home in San Diego accompanied by Chantell and my infant twin grandchildren, Bryce, and Brooklyn. I was thrilled to go back to work for the County and assume the oversight of regional child welfare, public health, and eligibility services.

As the assistant deputy director, I spent a substantial amount of time meeting with community partners. I enjoyed the diversity of my duties and the chance to collaborate with a cross-section of professionals inside and outside of my office.

Six months after our move, Alvin's unit deployed to Afghanistan in December of 2011. The demands of my new post kept me busy, and I needed the distraction to quell the anxiety I experienced because of his assignment to the Middle-East. Although we existed in different time zones, we stayed connected by using Face Time each night and exchanging emails several times a day.

When my boss directed me to expand my previous work implementing the Gallup organization's leadership model throughout the region, I welcomed the additional tasks. Not only did I want to stay busy, it was gratifying to observe the transformative nature of the training and to witness the growth and maturation of the supervisors and managers. As I learned more about the importance of culture and strategy within organizations, in February of 2012 I decided to apply to the Doctor of Management program at the University of Phoenix.

The road to obtaining my doctorate was paved with excitement, stress, and hard work all rolled into one. I buried myself in the process of moving through the doctoral program with a goal of graduating within four years. I developed a routine to meet my work and school obligations, averaging six hours of sleep per night.

My boss announced her retirement in 2013, and the agency director appointed me to serve as the director of regional operations. The expansion of my duties included the supervision of twelve hundred employees who provided services to the public in the eastern and northern regions of San Diego County. Simultaneous to the promotion I began my second year of the doctoral program and tried my best to flourish both in school and at work.

Every month the county chief administrative officer convened a meeting with one hundred and sixty department heads who managed the work of eighteen thousand county employees. She requested that I make a presentation to the group describing the implementation of the Gallup initiatives within the county. Later, she recognized four of my colleagues and me for our exceptional accomplishments related to designing and implementing an automated document processing system. My confidence was building, and I believed that my commitment to my employees and the community was evident.

In December of 2015, I received a call from a recruiter who wanted to gauge my interest in applying for a position in Riverside County, which was located sixty miles from San Diego. Based on his description of the needs of the department, the potential to serve as the assistant director of the children's services division piqued my interest.

The year 2016 marked a turning point in my career and my educational endeavors. I completed the requirements for my doctorate in January and passed my oral defense in early February. At the end of February, I participated in a panel interview in Riverside County with the director of the department of social services, the assistant county administrative officer, and the chief probation officer. After the interview, the director extended an offer of employment and I accepted the position with Alvin's blessings. I planned to make the one-hour commute daily from San Diego to Riverside County.

I started my new position in April and glided across the stage in the University of Phoenix Stadium in Phoenix, Arizona, to be awarded my diploma in May. Alvin, Chantell, Bryce, and Brooklyn rooted for me in the stands. My heart pounded as the president of the university adjusted my doctoral hood, and I resisted the urge to drop to my knees and shout *hallelujah*.

Throughout my time in Riverside County, I established new benchmarks for excellence with a focus on the success and engagement of employees. During my first year I re-structured the entire department and instituted protocols that reduced the attrition rate from 19 percent to 11.9 percent. I again worked with the Gallup organization to develop a training curriculum for the entire department of public social services. I served on several statewide committees and made contributions to the development of initiatives that have since been implemented.

I resigned my position in Riverside County in March of 2019, with the goal of taking a break from the emotional toll of working in the field of child welfare. The endless days of dealing with secondary trauma because of the maltreatment of children and the pernicious political environment caused me to consider early retirement.

Four months later, in July of 2019, I accepted a job as the chief operating officer for the Urban Corps of San Diego County. This organization provided a second chance for at-risk youth ages 18 to 22 years old who were seeking to earn a high school diploma while participating in a paid job training program.

Some of the youths were raised in the foster care system. Others served time in jail for various offenses or were homeless and living in their vehicles. Many were parents or tasked with the responsibility of financially caring for members of their family. I empathized with the youth served by the Urban Corps, and I tried to ensure that they had access to resources such as housing referrals, food, childcare, and counseling if needed. Today, I maintain contact with several of the youth who have graduated from the program and offer my support as requested.

During my tenure, representatives from the San Diego Business Journal selected me as a finalist for the *Business Woman of the Year* award. Although I did not win the award, I appreciated the acknowledgment of my contributions as the chief operating officer. I remained in the role until my resignation in June of 2021.

When I think about the thirty-eight years of service that I have provided to communities across the nation during my career as human services professional, I smile knowing that my parents would be impressed with the trajectory of my career. Traveling with Alvin to his various military assignments gave me exposure to organizations with different operational patterns and settings. The culture of some of the entities for which I worked were innovative, others could be classified as detrimental to one's health.

Whether my takeaways were positive or negative, I gleaned information that I could use to improve my knowledge from each system for which I was employed. My identity is tied to my life as a public servant. I took pleasure in advocating for and obtaining equitable resources for children, adults, and families.

Each position I held played an important part in shaping my sense of belonging. Although career accomplishments do not erase anger, shame, and self-doubt, my contributions to humankind elevated my awareness of my self-worth.

There is comfort in comfort,
however, to grow you must stretch yourself
and seek opportunities to maximize your strengths.

CHAPTER TWENTY-FIVE

My Ancestry

> *We're all ghosts.*
> *We all carry, inside us,*
> *people who came before us.*
>
> ~ Liam Callanan

In 2019, I decided to register on the Ancestry.com website to learn more about my family history. I knew many of my relatives on my dad's side of the family. However, I had almost no knowledge of my mom's lineage. My mom was the only child of my grandmother, Lillie Mae.

I recalled a limited amount of information about my grandmother. She traveled from Georgia to North Carolina to stay with us for weeks at a time after my mom left. My grandmother had a close relationship with my dad, and she cooked, cleaned, and did her best to fill in for my mom.

I remembered meeting some of my cousins when I attended my grandmother's funeral services in 1979, so I knew that I had cousins and extended relatives on my mom's side.

I created a profile on Ancestry.com and added as much information as possible so that I could find any members of my family. Through exploring my mom's background, I wanted to understand her history and find out more about her childhood.

Within a week of receiving my genetic profile, I checked the information on Ancestry.com and learned that I had more than one hundred second, third, and fourth cousins who shared a match with my results.

Before I had the opportunity to contact any of the connections, a call came through on my cell phone from a second cousin named Kim, a retired educator who resided in Atlanta, Georgia. She was four years older than I, and we had not met before. However, the first time we spoke the conversation flowed easily, and it seemed as though we had known each other for a long time.

We determined that we were related on my mom's side of the family. Our moms grew up together in Albany, Georgia. We exchanged notes about our current lives, and she gave me information about both my mom and my grandma. The conversation lasted for more than two hours.

Much to my dismay, I learned that my great-grandmother abandoned my grandmother, Lillie Mae and my great-uncle when they were children. Extended members of my great-grandmother's family raised them into adulthood. My mom never disclosed this information to me.

When my great-grandmother left her children, she moved to the next town to work as a domestic. From my understanding, my grandmother didn't hear from her mother again until nearly forty years later. At this point her health had declined and her long-term employer contacted my grandmother to inform her that she needed to secure a place to stay for her mother.

My cousin told me that my grandmother begrudgingly took her mother into her home, but she resented caring for her. I understood her hesitation, and I am unsure if I would have been able to do the same given the circumstances.

As I mulled over the timeline, I realized that my great-grandmother was alive and living with my grandmother up until she passed away in 1979. Insofar as I recall, my great-grandmother did not attend her funeral. It is astonishing to know that my siblings and I were unaware that she had reentered our grandmother's life and my mom never mentioned a word.

Speaking to my cousin, I realized that the impacts of multi-generational trauma affected the choices my parents made throughout their own lives. It is probable that the abandonment of both my grandmother and my dad influenced their psychological well-being. I began to view the lives of my mom and my dad through a different lens.

During our next conversation, Kim and I fast-forwarded to catching up about our families, our careers, and our siblings. By this time my sisters Gwen and Joyce had passed, and she had few memories of my sister Mary. When she asked about my brothers, I updated her about Arthur Jr., Patrick, and Edward.

She spoke of playing with Edward as a child because my grandmother raised him until she sent him to live with us in North Carolina at the age of 15. The conversation stalled, and Kim was quiet for a few moments before we moved on to another topic.

The next day Kim sent me a text asking to speak to me about an incident involving Edward that had happened during her childhood. I replied, *I suppose that you want to tell me that Edward has been preying on little girls for quite some time.*

Within minutes my cell phone rang. When I answered I listened as Kim recounted a story about when she was 8 years old, and Edward pinned her up against the wall and tried to fondle her through her underwear. Edward was 12 years old, but she managed to push him away and avoided being around him outside of the presence of adults thereafter.

Kim stated that she had never discussed the episode with her mom or other members of her family. She assimilated the incident in her mind and never mentioned it to anyone.

The realization that Edward's predatory behavior hadn't originated with me shook me to my core.

At the age of 12, Edward acted in a sexually aggressive way toward our cousin. Based on my work in child welfare, I was familiar with the phenomenon of the victim-to-perpetrator cycle, a notion that those who have been sexually victimized as children might commit acts against others later in their lives.

Edward's arrival in North Carolina at the age of 15 now made sense. I considered the likelihood that he also might have been a victim of abuse. I will never know if this is true, as I am unwilling to converse with him regarding the issue. A confirmation of my suspicion at this point has no value; an affirmative response on his part would not excuse his conduct.

I pondered whether my mom or my grandmother had knowledge of inappropriate behaviors that he exhibited toward others or if he was molested. It is possible that they both knew and wanted to keep it hidden. Through my writing I strive to convey the message that each of us has a responsibility to break down the walls of intergenerational secrets.

I created an account on Ancestry.com to learn more about my family history and connect with my extended family. What I gained, though, was an absolute resolve to make sure that my grandchildren and my nieces and nephews are shielded from the generational curses that seem to reside in my genetic makeup.

CHAPTER TWENTY-SIX

Me Too, and You, and Him, and Her

> *Abuse is a parasite that feeds off of hate*
> *and shame, growing in size*
> *and strength with silence.*
>
> ~ Nikki Sex

In 2006, Tarana Burke, a survivor and activist founded the *me too* movement to build a network of resources to combat sexual violence. In 2017, the hashtag #metoo went viral in response to revelations of sexual harassment and assault in the entertainment industry.

Twitter users in the United States and across the world tweeted the #metoo hashtag more than a million and half times while Facebook users posted the hashtag more than twelve million times. These actions confirmed the pervasive nature of sexual abuse in our society.

Childhood sexual abuse owns a rightful place in the movement. Sexual abuse of children has been veiled in the fabric of society for centuries dating back to the Middle Ages. It is my hope that the momentum generated by the renewed interest in sexual assault re-awakens the awareness that we must all work together to protect the girls and boys who have resorted to hiding in the closet at a family member's home or in the bathroom at their church to escape their abuser. But the fact that the awareness surrounding the predominance of sexual abuse appeared to increase when the perpetrators were identified as high-profile, rich men was alarming.

The U.S. Department of Health and Human Services (2010) reported that more than seventy thousand children were sexually abused in 2008. Finkelhor et al., (2010) published data that indicated that one in five girls and one in twenty boys are victimized as children.

Research conducted by Hanson et al., (2003) posited that nearly one in three victims of sexual assault never reported their encounter, and due to victim blaming and embarrassment, many children did not disclose molestation until adulthood. The silence often resulted in depression, anxiety, substance abuse, and an infinite number of physiological disorders.

A Bureau of Justice Statistics research report found that children are least likely to be sexually abused by strangers (2010). Most perpetrators of sexual abuse are family members. The information provided by Finkelhor and his colleagues also indicated that children who are victimized develop low self-esteem, feelings of worthlessness, and an abnormal view of sexual intimacy.

Statistics suggest that the prevalence of sexual abuse is the same in Black families as it is in Caucasian families. Yet, Black families are less apt to involve the police in cases of childhood sexual abuse due to the fear of embarrassment, financial implications, and breaking up the family structure (Stone, 2004). As a result, many victims dealt with the impacts of sexual abuse in isolation.

Wyatt stated that half of Black female victims never disclosed being a survivor of childhood sexual abuse (1997). When I wrote a speech entitled *Getting To My Enough* to present to a focus group in 2016, I asked six of my closest Black girlfriends to read the speech before I presented it.

To my amazement, five of the women revealed to me that family members had sexually abused them when they were children. As in my case, they continued to interact with the perpetrator after the abuse. Three of the women never discussed their experience with any adults and described their worry at the possibility of being ostracized by their family. In the other two cases, adults knew about the molestation but remained silent, leaving each of my friends to believe that she was to blame for the abuse.

By not confronting the exploiters and yet believing that the abuse that the victims reported transpired, some adults are either knowingly or unknowingly complicit in condoning the molestation. Coupled with the cultural message that Black women are perceived as strong, many adults who are aware of the occurrences of sexual abuse are deficient in knowing how to address the situation.

As a perpetrator of sexual abuse, Edward received permission to return to my family home at the age of 25. From my perspective as a child, the decision to agree for Edward to live in my family home sent a clear message to me that my safety did not matter. I choose to believe now that the message was inadvertent and instead resulted from my dad's lack of understanding about the lifelong impacts of abuse.

I normalized my continued interactions with Edward until my mid-forties by blocking out the past and behaving as though our relationship was that of a typical sister and brother. As adults, I permitted him to spend the night in my home. My body floods with guilt knowing that I exposed my daughter to an abuser. I am disheartened that I didn't cut off my interactions with Edward as soon as I reached adulthood.

Suffering in silence is not an indication of strength. The romanticizing of the strong Black woman persona has contributed to the epidemic of mental illness. Normally, childhood sexual abuse victims do not have a media platform to discuss their cases and the ensuing trauma. Therefore, it is imperative for each of us to learn how to initiate uncomfortable conversations about abuse of any type, anxiety, depression, and the urge to harm oneself.

Breaking the generational cycle of abuse must be done purposefully. Victims of childhood sexual abuse deserve to receive trauma-informed care with a focus on healing and resilience. Without treatment, unaddressed childhood trauma may compromise relationships in adulthood.

The reaction to the #metoo movement confirmed that a person does not have to be a multi-millionaire or a media mogul to have power. The power could simply be held by five-foot, four-inch-tall, 160-pound man who appears as a giant to a 7-year-old child.

Becoming Dr. Marie

Everything was done for the first time at some point,

go ahead and take a chance at succeeding.

CHAPTER TWENTY-SEVEN

Black, Female, and Scared, But Not Angry

We are all broken.
That's how the light gets in.

~ Ernest Hemingway

The trauma that I endured as a child shaped my behavior in my adult life. I learned to present myself as strong, assertive, and confident. At times, my disposition has been misperceived as aggressive, arrogant, and angry. In retrospect, I understand how the label of the *angry Black woman* could have been applied to me. Yet, I wasn't angry. I was scared, and I was scarred.

There is a body of research that explores the myths surrounding the angry Black woman. Negative tropes in American culture include the description of Black women as ignorant, bad-tempered, and hostile (Ashley, 2014). Made famous by the show Amos and Andy in the 1930s, Sapphire, a Black character, was portrayed as rude, overbearing, and angry in general. The Sapphire stereotype has influenced the ways in which white Americans view Black women. Conversely, white women have been characterized as pure with indisputable moral character (Hernandez & Rehman, 2002). Other studies have indicated that Black women are perceived as more threatening than white women (Accapadi, 2007).

By circumstance, Black women have been required to be strong, tough, and independent and too many times have served as the head of the household. Throughout times past, Black women have been the main source of support for their families and the caregivers for their children while working inside and outside the home. Black women have also shouldered the emotional burden that often accompanies caring for broken Black men.

In my professional realm as a Black female, I managed the unbalanced expectations that existed for me and my white counterparts. Lynn reported that Black women compete in the workplace for recognition, promotions, equal pay, and sometimes just to be heard (2019). The author also stated that often a perception exists that Black women believe that they are not respected and are beset by the need to defend their actions, words, and decisions.

According to an opinion article written in 2014 in *Blavity News*, when Black women voiced any type of displeasure in a work environment they were defined as hostile and labeled as intimidating. Instead of being perceived as proposing a valuable opinion, Black women reported being the subject of harsh judgment. They also reported that they were expected to have a more calm and reserved response to appear acceptable to their colleagues.

In some of my work environments, I had the sense that I could be successful to a certain extent. What some people mistook for arrogance and cockiness was really anxiety that I would make a mistake and be punished for doing so.

As a Black leader, I had many firsts. In Louisiana, for the department of children and family services, I served as the first Black chief of staff.

In San Diego County I was the second Black person and the first Black female to serve as a regional general manager, and in Riverside County I became the first Black assistant director of public social services. I assumed the role of chief operating officer for the Urban Corps of San Diego County as the first Black female to do so.

Blazing the trail to earn these positions required tenacity, political acumen, and tolerance. Practicing the three Ps, prayer, patience, and perseverance, was vital to remaining in them.

In past roles, I acknowledge that I felt invisible on occasion. For example, while partnering on a special project with white colleagues, some people attempted to talk over me during a meeting and rejected my recommendations. I asserted myself in the meeting by speaking in a direct and firm tone.

Later, my supervisor informed me that my colleagues expressed discomfort and concern about my *behavior*. Her statement offended me. My perspective is that having a frank style of communication and being angry do not have the same meaning. However, I decided to examine the ways in which my tone might contribute to perpetuating the myth of the angry Black woman.

After the episode I consulted with my mentor. She suggested that I soften my tone and lower my voice during meetings. Initially, I resisted changing my style in order to be accepted by my peers. Then, I realized that advancing my emotional intelligence would be beneficial to my growth as a leader.

To meet my goal of reaching an executive level position, I needed to demonstrate the ability to effectively engage my peers. Although it may be easy to *accept* the reasons why some Black women are perceived as angry, it is not *acceptable* for us to let the perception of that anger to stagnate our ascension to greatness.

For some of my colleagues or subordinate staff, changing my tone of voice didn't reduce their level of uneasiness. But, I have learned that I am not responsible for the anxieties of others, I am only responsible for presenting a professional demeanor at all times. More importantly, when I speak I am doing so from a place of assurance knowing that I earned my place based on my knowledge, background, and education.

In part, the motivation to further my education derived from the desire to earn credentials to compete in the workplace. More than 95 percent of my colleagues on the executive leadership teams in California, Texas, and Louisiana were white. At least 75 percent of them had less education and experience than I do.

My purpose for discussing this topic is not to invalidate all of the myths surrounding the perception of the angry Black woman. Nor is my intention to validate the labels that we involuntarily wear because others may be frightened by our legacy as a population of fierce, resourceful, and determined individuals.

I will, however, discuss the opportunities that we have to change the labels and opinions that *precede* us and *impede* our path to victory. We can each work to dispel the existing false narratives and use our talents to achieve the dreams and goals that we have set for ourselves.

Black women have made countless contributions to society. The load that we carry is heavy, and I encourage others to choose now as the time to release the burden that we have continued to haul around for our ancestors. Only then may we hope that we are setting an example for the next generation of women.

I don't want to sugarcoat the fact that the myth of the angry Black woman will remain in the minds of many. Perhaps our real or perceived anger is a justifiable response to the cards that we have been dealt by society.

Nevertheless, as a former executive leader who was being lauded as a role model for Black and Brown employees across the organizations for which I worked, I made the decision that my actions would demonstrate that Black women are enough, that we are equal, and that we are competent. My hope is that the future state of society will be free of the myth that Black women are loud, overbearing, stubborn, and sometimes malicious.

I would be remiss if I didn't mention the barriers that Black women create between and amongst each other. When a Black woman is angry at another Black woman and labels her the same way that we complain about being described by others, it is damaging. We should assume the role of uplifting and supporting each other; by doing so we could create a society that is accustomed to valuing our heritage.

Is your fear of failure keeping you from being great?

It is okay to start over

and make adjustments along the way.

There are no failures,

just lessons to develop a strategy.

CHAPTER TWENTY-EIGHT

Am I an Imposter?

> *You can never be overdressed*
> *or overeducated.*
>
> ~ Oscar Wilde

Despite the periods of inner turmoil, I enjoyed many successes in my professional career. Yet, I remained restless and unfulfilled. I cerebrally searched for a mystical solution that would quiet the voices that told me that the successes in my life were still lacking.

Earning a doctorate signifies mastery in a certain field, and less than 1.2 percent of the population in the United States possesses this degree. I envisioned that upon earning my doctorate my jubilation would overflow and that I would experience a mental transformation. That didn't happen, the restlessness continued.

Throughout my tenure working in San Diego County, I mentored female employees and coached them with respect to their educational and professional goals. My reason for deciding to mentor women began because of my understanding of how aspirations could be stifled by private inner battles. I desired to motivate and support women and provide them with the tools to advance in their careers.

The women I mentored assumed that my life was ideal, and they often articulated their admiration for my endeavors. On the surface I appeared successful and content in the eyes of others. But, even though I wore designer clothes and shoes and drove high-end cars, I dealt with low self-esteem.

The residual trauma from my past manifested in many ways. I questioned my capacity as a leader even when my superiors and colleagues showered me with accolades for my work. My lack of belief in myself subconsciously paralyzed me at times.

My fear that I wasn't *enough*, powered me to strive to do better to the point of exhaustion. I silently berated my performance even as I received awards for the initiatives that I designed.

Throughout my career, in the majority of my senior level positions, I found myself surrounded by white colleagues. In California, less than 1 percent of my contemporaries in senior leadership roles were Black. This was not attributable to the demographics, but rather to the fact that few Black associates advanced to the executive level in the county. This fact increased my uneasiness and I believed that judgments were made about my abilities based on the color of my skin.

Over time, I realized that I suffered from a phenomenon known as the Imposter Syndrome. According to Brevata et al., (2019), the Imposter Syndrome refers to an individual's belief that he or she is not as competent as perceived by others despite evidence of his or her skills and knowledge. Upon reading the definition of the term for the first time, I recognized that the description represented who I had been for so many years.

During my undergraduate and graduate degree programs I worked and went to school full time. I tried to earn perfect grades in every class. For me, excelling in school would signify that I could be successful. My attempts to overcompensate for my worries were the precursor for my underlying stress.

I decided that I needed to clear my mind of the negative energy that originated with the shame that I absorbed as a result of being molested. To begin the process of healing, my internal thoughts had to match my external demeanor. By learning how to release the shame and positively affirm myself, I could gain liberation from the belief that I contributed to Edward's behavior.

You

Are

Enough!

CHAPTER TWENTY-NINE

It Doesn't Always Have to Be Perfect

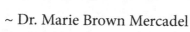

*Eternal love begins
with being a mother.*

~ Dr. Marie Brown Mercadel

Chantell is an excellent mother, and at a glance she seems to be much like me, an assertive thinker, driven, strong, and independent. From the moment that Bryce and Brooklyn were born in April of 2011, Chantell and I snapped photos by the hundreds since we knew how fast they would grow up.

One time, as Chantell readied the camera to catch a particular expression on Brooklyn's face, I let out a loud gasp. *Wait! I need to check my hair.*

I will never forget Chantell's reaction to my overreaction. *Mom, you don't always have to be perfect, as if you just stepped out of the pages of Vogue magazine.*

Although it may seem odd, Chantell's declaration awakened me to the realization that even in my forties I still aimed to appear as though

I was impeccable to fit in with life. As I selectively chose the pictures to post on social media, I tried to present my best self to the world. I seldom left the house without a perfect hairstyle, a coordinated outfit, and impeccable make-up.

Knowing that Chantell perceived that I needed every aspect of my life to appear *perfect* forced me to reflect. I wondered if I had unconsciously sent a message to her throughout her life that she needed to live without making mistakes.

My dread is that, in trying to be a role model for her, I sent a message that she wasn't good enough. When she communicated that she believed that she was a disappointment to me, I cried. I explained to her that not only did she make me proud; she inspired me to thrive and embark on the path to healing.

Many elements of the conversation caused my heart to ache. I now recognize that Chantell has spent a great deal of time in her life trying to please me and live up to the standards that she perceives that I hold.

Of course, I wish that I had made some different decisions as a parent. In her early years I sacrificed our time together while pursuing my career and educational aspirations. As a single parent, I made the choices that I believed would help us to live comfortably as a family.

I wanted to have the means for Chantell to participate in extracurricular activities, travel, live in a home in a safe neighborhood, and get an excellent education. If I could step back into the 1990s, I would work to create a reasonable balance between the nurturing of my daughter and meeting my life goals.

Going forward I am dedicated to ensuring that the current messages that I convey to Chantell, Brooklyn, and the other women in my family are clear.

I will teach them to strive to reach their self-defined level of contentment instead of aiming to meet the standards of others. This is a lesson that I wish that my mom had taught to me.

My relationship with Chantell has gone through similar cycles that play out in many mother-daughter relationships. I applaud the way in which she has handled the ebbs and flows in her life. She is one of my biggest cheerleaders, and she has shown me grace and patience. Although we don't always agree on certain topics, I rely on her for advice, and I value her opinion.

With every lesson

comes an opportunity

to grow…

CHAPTER THIRTY

Melanie, Release Yourself

> *At some point in a woman's life,*
> *she just gets tired of being ashamed all the*
> *time. After that, she is free to become what-*
> *ever she truly is.*
>
> ~ Elizabeth Gilbert

I am not harder on any other single person on the planet than I am on myself. After thinking over Chantell's previous declaration about my need to be perfect, I admitted to myself that, throughout adulthood, I have critiqued every aspect of my existence, including my appearance, my intelligence, my career, my decisions, and other facets of my life. The overthinking and analyzing of my actions at times has been crushing to the point of exhaustion. Even when I was doing fine, I still believed that I should be doing better.

The funny part is, though, that I hardly realized that I unconsciously evaluated myself in real time. On too many occasions to count in my work life, I normalized questioning whether I deserved to be in a room full of executives who seemed to bring more knowledge than I had to the discussion.

Somehow, I overlooked the fact that not only did I earn the right to be in my position; my educational background and proficiency level exceeded those of many of the people who sat beside me.

I have learned over time that trauma may have a deleterious effect on an individual's self-esteem. Regardless of when the trauma occurs, the residual outcomes often manifest in a variety of ways during adulthood. Like me, many people are unable to make the connection between their present behaviors and their past experiences.

I cannot use the rationale that my childhood trauma was the reason that I have made some serious mistakes in life. I take ownership for the things that I have done wrong, all my bad decisions, and the people whom I have hurt in the process.

At times I was physically present but emotionally unavailable and disconnected. During some periods I traveled through life operating as an empty vessel, and as a result, I know that I might have wounded others.

Internalizing this knowledge causes pain for me, and I have at times been ashamed of my actions. The psychological weight of the stories that we voice to ourselves when we are recovering from trauma is a heavy emotional load to carry.

I have spent countless hours mentoring other women, helping them to find their voice and their passions, and providing them with the tools necessary to mend. I often shared with them the treatment methods that worked for me. On occasion, I coached myself and my mentees at the same time, striving to heal the both of us by destroying and re-designing negative thought patterns. The process of giving back to others gave me a sense of comfort and peace.

Before I could absolve myself of my own embarrassment, blame, and anger, I needed to forgive the most important person in my life, me. By exercising the trifecta of mind, body, and spirit, I accepted that

I could consider my personal needs first. Doing so would not take away from my duties as a wife, a mother, a grandmother, a sister, an aunt, or a friend. Instead, I used my desire to embrace self-care as the foundations for me to become whole.

The traumatic events in my life also led me to tolerate people and circumstances when I should have exited unhealthy situations. The obstacles to overcoming trauma-related events are greater when people in your circle reinforce the negative perspectives that you are holding within. The process of cleansing and healing involves eliminating certain behaviors and people from your life. And sometimes it is easier to proclaim your intentions to do so than it is to execute the decision.

Fontes and Plummer indicated that a component of post traumatic stress disorder for survivors of sexual and physical abuse is caused by self-blame (2010). It is regrettable that we live in a culture that is shrouded in the belief that survivors play a role in their victimization by demonstrating certain behaviors, such as dressing provocatively or *sending mixed messages.*

In my case, when Edward received approval to return to our home and did not suffer any consequences for his actions, the belief that I deserved the abuse was reinforced in my mind. It would take close to forty-five years for me to process that I was a defenseless child who was not responsible for the actions of a troubled 18-year-old kid who was almost a man. He should have been my protector.

I have shifted the blame for his behavior from me to him. At this point in my life, I am stronger than I have ever been before.

Dreams without action
are merely hallucinations.

CHAPTER THIRTY-ONE

Thank You, Daddy

> *My dad was not perfect,*
> *and he didn't wear a cape,*
> *but he was my real-life hero.*
>
> ~ Dr. Marie Brown Mercadel

I have always had so much respect for my dad. Although he did not have an extensive formal education, he was well versed in many subject areas and enjoyed debating various topics. He lived in impoverished conditions as a child and suffered through parental abandonment. Yet, he had a strong work ethic and taught me and my siblings the value of self-discipline.

Prior to his enlistment in the United States Marine Corps in 1942, President Franklin D. Roosevelt signed an executive order that stated, in part, *...there shall be no discrimination in the employment of workers in the defense industries or government because of race, creed, color, or national origin.*

Still, the Black recruits who are known as the Montford Point Marines, endured blatant hostility and institutional bias during their enlistment. Although many of the Marines fought in World War II, they didn't garner the respect or recognition that they deserved.

Fast forward to seventy years after my father enlisted in the Marine Corps, and twenty-five years after his death, the United States Congress unanimously passed legislation that recognized the service of the Montford Point Marines with the Congressional Gold Medal of Honor for the service that they provided to this country. I was honored to attend the ceremony with my siblings to accept the award.

My admiration for my dad derives from the fact that in the 1970s it was unusual for a man to raise children as a single parent. My dad could have abandoned my siblings and me and sent us to languish in the foster care system, but his love for us prevented this from happening. He provided for all the necessities that my siblings and I required. I believe that my mom knew that my dad would make the needed sacrifices to support us and keep us together.

My dad was a no-nonsense kind of guy. He didn't like excuses. He wanted action. He often expected more effort from me than I thought I had to give.

We abided by numerous household rules, some of which I considered to be overkill. As children, we never spent the night at the homes of our friends. However, our friends could sleep over with us. My sisters were prohibited from dating boys unless my dad knew their parents.

I was aghast when my dad ordered Gwen and Joyce to accompany me to my eighth-grade prom and serve as hostesses. When I think about the rules now, I often chuckle at the depth of my dad's insight. At times, I participated in activities that were far outside the scope of what I should have been doing, and I deserved the strict monitoring.

My dad loved kids and helping every person he could. During my junior high school years in the late 1970s, I recall our home serving as the gathering place for many of the young boys in the neighborhood. My dad hosted oyster boils in the back yard, and folks always played a game of Spades.

My dad mentored and advised these young boys, many of whom were from single-parent households. He also had a long list of people whom he helped by loaning them money, buying groceries, and giving them rides as needed. My siblings and I grew accustomed to making room for children who initially came to our home for the weekend and ended up staying for months.

My current outlook on my life includes unconditional forgiveness for the way that my dad handled the situation with Edward. His intentions were pure. My belief lies in thinking that the fear of losing his children if child protective services investigated the allegations of abuse frightened him.

The path to forgiving my dad was an easy one for me. He didn't intend to hurt me. Instead, his love for me was undeniable. My observation of his generous nature with the members of our community became a driving force in my career as a public servant. For that, I will always be grateful.

Let your light shine
even when it appears that others
may want to dim the view for you.
Trust your instincts
and have faith in your abilities.

CHAPTER THIRTY-TWO

Mom, I Forgive You

> *But if you do not forgive others their sins,*
> *your father will not forgive your sins.*
>
> ~ Matthew 6:15

I often marvel at the photographs taken of my mom when she was younger in which she wore mini-skirts and sported an afro. Many of our friends and family tell me that we look alike, and that makes me joyful. I know that I inherited my heart to serve others from her. She introduced me to volunteer work and encouraged me to attend nursing school.

I finally started to come to grips with her departure from my life as a child after Chantell was born. I reasoned that she must have been overwhelmed by the condition of her life.

As a 16-year-old child she married a man twelve years her senior. My opinion on this matter is purely speculative, but it is my belief that as my mom grew older and started to mature, she recognized that she had very few things in common with my dad. By the time my mom left the marriage she was thirty-four years old and my dad was forty-six years old. I would imagine that as my dad was settling down after a successful military career, my mom might have been trying to discover who she wanted to become.

Although rearing large families is not atypical in the South, birthing seven children over the course of sixteen years would have been challenging in the best of circumstances. It is not my job to make excuses for my mom, but the gravity of her situation is understandable to me now.

She counted on reuniting with her children once she found a home and had the means to support us. She believed that my dad would eventually concede to her request for us to live with her in California. She misjudged his resolve for us to remain with him in North Carolina.

By the time she returned to Jacksonville in 1993, the window for mothering her children had closed. We were adults living our own lives and trying our best to pursue happiness. After my separation and subsequent divorce, we became much closer and spent quite a bit of time together. Although it is never possible to make up for lost time, I appreciated her efforts to help me as a single parent studying for my undergraduate degree. My rate of success would have been less if she had not been a part of my support system.

Prior to returning to Jacksonville, she became a registered nurse. She worked as a unit manager for Brynn Marr Psychiatric Center, a facility that served patients with mental health issues. We enjoyed exchanging information about best practices in the field and emerging treatment modalities.

A year before my mom died in 1996, she stayed in my home in Durham while attending a conference. Over dinner, I gained the courage to raise the subject of my molestation. Her reaction was one of outrage. She adamantly denied having any knowledge of the abuse. I erroneously assumed that my dad informed her of Edward's actions. My realization that she was hearing this information for the first time stunned me.

My mom's disbelief provided clarity for why she never inquired about the incidents or expressed any concern about my well-being. She evaded the discussion and retreated to the bedroom, further reinforcing my thoughts of shame. To my knowledge, my mom never confronted my brother about my allegations. I never discussed the molestation with her again.

It is easy to dwell on the *what ifs* in life. However, I have always wondered if I might have started the healing process as a child if my dad was transparent with my mom and they prevented Edward from returning to our home.

If my mom and dad completed the ACES questionnaire today, they would both answer affirmatively to more than five questions. The more I understand the research surrounding multi-generational trauma, the more empathetic I am to the experiences that each of my parents lived through.

I love my mom, I forgive her, and I am grateful for the life lessons that she taught me. I miss her every day, and I wish that she could see that the dreams that she had for my life have come true.

Do not waste your time on things or people
who are not bringing positive energy
into your life.

CHAPTER THIRTY-THREE

My Sisters, My Keepers

> *Sisters are a gift from God.*
> *They will wipe your tears, hold your hand*
> *and kick your butt too.*
>
> ~ Dr. Marie Brown Mercadel

B eing the youngest of four girls may be a gift or a curse. As a child I followed behind Gwen, Joyce, and Mary trying to figure out what they were doing. I also schemed to borrow their clothes, their shoes, their earrings, and other items that I thought I wanted to use. Sometimes my relentless begging worked, and sometimes it didn't. My sisters would likely classify me as an annoying and overly talkative pest.

The relationship I had with each of my sisters was different. Gwen filled the role of my mom and our connection resembled one more like that of mother and daughter. As I aged, she became my best friend, and I was protective of her.

She sacrificed much of her own life to care for me and my siblings. I believe that she failed to recover from the trauma of our mom's absence and never had the true opportunity to attain her personal goals in life.

She loved to sketch. She enrolled in art classes for a time and dreamed of drawing pictures and displaying them in an art gallery. When she married in 1980, her husband moved into the family home so that she could care for my dad when he became ill. She worked at Onslow Memorial Hospital as a certified nursing assistant for more than twenty-five years. I admonished her for giving more of herself to others and neglecting her own health.

Gwen had a heart of gold, and when we were together in the community people who knew her stopped to hug her and thank her for the compassion shown to them or for a relative during their hospitalization.

No matter in which state I lived, I flew or drove back to North Carolina to visit her two or three times a year. We spoke on the telephone daily. While smiling from ear-to-ear, she stood next to me and continuously snapped pictures when I graduated with both my bachelor's and master's degrees.

My world changed in 2006 when she suffered a fatal heart attack at the age of 51. On June 18th, which also happened to be Mary's 47th birthday, I answered an early morning telephone call from Chantell. She had spent the weekend with Gwen, but she is not an early riser, so I immediately knew that something was wrong. When I picked up the line Chantell's screams were so loud that I could hardly decipher what she was saying. When she finally calmed down to tell me that Gwen was found kneeling against the chair in the den dead, I stumbled around in a stupor.

I already had a flight scheduled to North Carolina on June 21st to attend our annual family picnic. Instead of going to my native home to roast a pig and cook the traditional picnic fixings with our friends, the purpose of my trip changed to planning a funeral to bury my sister.

When I close my eyes, I can still see her smile, and I hear her say, *I am so happy for you, Melanie.* I keep a chest full of greeting cards that she sent me over the years. Each of the messages in the cards was supportive and uplifting, and the handwritten notes contained language encouraging me to live my dreams.

One birthday gift that she gave me, a statue with the inscription, *I love you because you lift me up when I hit bottom,* sits on my nightstand. It is the first image that I see in the morning and the last image that I see each night. I take comfort in keeping old mementos near me.

Sixteen years later the sting of her death remains, but I find joy in reading the cards that she sent me and rubbing the statue and the inspirational quote. These acts help me keep her spirit alive.

My sister Joyce could be described as a firecracker; she openly spoke her mind and didn't mince any words. I referred to her as my alter ego because she would say things out loud that I only thought about in my head. When angry, she could glare at a person in a manner that would make them feel as though a dagger pierced their entire body. If she liked an individual, she would offer him or her the shirt off her back. If she didn't like someone, she didn't hide her disdain.

One of my favorite memories of her involved her taking me, my brother Patrick, and my niece Pam to the movies every Sunday. Going to the theatre became the highlight of my week. During our conversations as adults, I could be honest with my thoughts, and she never judged me for my shortcomings. She visited me often in California, and we always spent Thanksgiving together.

Joyce suffered from lupus, an autoimmune disease that attacks tissues and organs. She retired on disability from her job as a certified nursing assistant in 2008. However, she continued to provide home health services to older adults throughout the community.

I knew that she was in pain on most days, and I wanted to assist her so that she could stop working. Fiercely independent, she refused to accept most of the financial help that I offered. When the lupus flare-ups occurred and she required hospitalization for treatment, I flew to North Carolina to confer with her medical team.

Joyce preferred to keep the details of her condition private and didn't always tell the truth about the severity of her illness. She neglected to reveal all the information that was given by her doctor, and I knew that she didn't want me to worry about her health. On more than one occasion, I surprised her with my arrival in North Carolina to accompany her to her doctor's appointments.

At one visit, I learned that the lupus was far more advanced than she had ever acknowledged. Again, I offered to provide her with financial assistance so that she could leave her job, but she declined. I respected her desire to maintain her independence and continue to work, but I knew that the type of tasks that she performed for her patients could exacerbate her illness.

One week prior to a trip to Barcelona, Spain that Alvin and I had planned in October of 2016, Joyce experienced a lupus flare-up and sought treatment at the hospital. She called me upon admittance and stated that she would be discharged after a forty-eight-hour course of treatment with intravenous steroids.

Alvin and I considered cancelling our trip if her health worsened. She sounded tired, which I expected, but my instincts led me to believe that I needed to see her in person. Forty-eight hours later I flew to North Carolina to visit and speak to her doctor about her condition.

The doctor informed me that she would recover but stated that she would require outpatient treatment to stabilize her blood sugar levels and manage her discomfort.

Once the doctor assured me that her illness could be managed, I returned to California. We decided to move forward with our vacation, and I planned to spend a week with Joyce when I returned. Four days into our trip Chantell called us and told us that Joyce had sepsis and an infection had spread throughout her body. Her lungs were failing, and the doctors had made the decision to put her on a ventilator, a device that acts as a breathing machine.

Alvin and I flew from Spain to North Carolina, and we requested a meeting with the medical team and our family, including Joyce's husband, Frankie, and her daughter, Kaminisha. The doctors told us that the infection was too far advanced and that the treatment options had been exhausted. We needed to decide if we wanted to remove her from the ventilator, which would result in her passing within an hour. We made the excruciating decision to disconnect all devices, and she passed away surrounded by her friends and family.

Some people say that God knows best and that he doesn't make any mistakes, but my heart was broken again. I fought through anxiety and depression after her death. Yet, I knew that her days of living in pain had ended. I also knew that she expected me to move forward and live my life to the fullest.

My sister Mary is six years older than I am. We didn't spend a lot of time together as children because she was hardly ever at home. She spent as much time as my dad allowed on the go with her friends. Darkskinned with pretty, long, black hair that she wore in an afro, I always admired her beauty and her sense of fashion.

Mary was 22 years old and living in New York City when I moved to California during high school. When I returned to North Carolina to live in 1987, she was 29 years old, and we rarely saw each other. She had a son, a career, and her own family to keep her busy.

Through our grieving Joyce's death, Mary and I have established a relationship that continues to tighten. We speak on the telephone at least twice daily to keep up with the events in the neighborhood and to chat in general.

Mary is the type of sister who will go to war for her siblings. She has a reputation for being tough, and she wouldn't hesitate to engage in a physical fight if necessary. She is also kind-hearted and sensitive, a side of her that she would rather keep hidden.

We often laugh about the time that she made me smell ammonia in an attempt to kill me or the time that she purposely burned my scalp with the straightening comb out of anger because my dad made her do my hair. Of course, her recollection of these events is different from mine.

I am grateful for our relationship. I am the younger sister, but at times I am compelled to treat her as though I am the older sister. Sometimes she takes my advice, and sometimes she ignores me. Such is the dynamic of our relationship, but I love her dearly.

There is uniqueness in the bonds that I had or have with each of my sisters. In many ways, they paved the way for me to be the person I am today. They scolded me, molded me, prayed for me, and encouraged me. My sisters have been my keepers throughout my entire life. Without the influence of each one of them, my status in life could have been different. Absent their love and guidance, I may never have made it through the process of *getting to my enough.*

CHAPTER THIRTY-FOUR

We Still Do

> *Marriage is like a house. When a light bulb*
> *goes out, you do not go and buy a*
> *new house, you fix the light bulb.*
>
> *~ Happy Wives Club*

Twenty-seven years after Alvin and I first met, and twenty-five years of marriage later, we still *say I do*. It is no secret that we have weathered storms in our marriage; it has taken a significant amount of work for us to stay together.

Serving in the military for thirty years is hard, completing a dissertation is hard, and being a parent is hard. Staying married with an intact relationship for twenty-five years is miraculous.

When two people get married and recite the section of the vows *"for better or worse"*, they have no idea exactly what they are agreeing to withstand. Ngina Otiende, a popular marriage therapist quoted, *"marriage is meant to keep people together, not just when things are good, but particularly when they are not. That's why we take marriage vows, not wishes"*.

Every marriage scenario is different and the path for managing adversity in a relationship is solely dependent upon the desires of the two parties that are involved. While Alvin's affair ruptured our initial foundation, we created new expectations for restoring trust and starting over.

I forgive Alvin for hurting me. Not only that, I emancipated myself from any thoughts that the affair happened because I was lacking in any area. I respect the fact that he took responsibility for caring for his daughter and that he loves her unconditionally. I have spent time with her and attended important events in her life such as her college graduation.

Though he and I were not blessed with children of our own, we are actively engaged with Bryce and Brooklyn. We enjoy traveling with them, exploring new restaurants, supporting their extracurricular activities such as Tae Kwon Do and gymnastics, and watching movies together. To them, he is Papa and I am Mimi, and these are the best titles we have ever earned.

We have accomplished a great deal together and we did so because we believed in the power of our love. We will continue to grow, flourish, and create memories together.

CHAPTER THIRTY-FIVE

Overcoming the Blockages

> *For whatever it is worth, it is never too late*
> *to be whoever you want to be. I hope that*
> *you live a life that you are proud of, and if*
> *you find that you are not, I hope that you*
> *have the strength to start over.*
>
> ~ Unknown

In January of 2020 I penned the first five pages of this book. Based on my work schedule, I set a goal to write a minimum of one paragraph a day, when the time was available. I knew in advance that putting my thoughts on paper, dealing with flashbacks, and replaying the scenarios I wrote about would extend the process of completing my manuscript. As I pondered the possible contents of the book, my thoughts whirled with misgivings about moving forward with my writing.

Some days I wrote ten or twelve paragraphs, other times I didn't write for a month. I underestimated how the flood of memories, fear of judgment, and the potential for hurting others with my revelations would interrupt my goal.

Reminiscing conjured up an excess of sentiments, some of which I was unprepared to re-live. I wasn't sure if every aspect of my life should be revealed. I knew that Alvin, our daughters, as well as my grandchildren, siblings, and friends would read this book.

As my level of indecision increased, I sought encouragement from Chantell and Alvin and talked through my reluctance. After these conversations, I decided to proceed and fight through the blockages. Nonetheless, the uncertainty remained.

Some of my experiences have driven me to the place at which I have arrived today. However, I expect that components of my story could result in anything from mild repercussions to some serious backlash. Some people might judge me and my decision to openly describe my story. Others might use my story as a motivational tool to help address their own internal strife.

Writing my memoir is cathartic for me. Much of what I have written on these pages is to help me release the inner thoughts that often lurk in the back of my mind. I hope that my words will be used as a vehicle to touch the lives of other women and assist them in *getting to their enough.*

I believe that I must share this story to heal myself, which then serves as a means to help others. My goal is to encourage people to release the strain of the guilt that is too often stomached by survivors of sexual abuse.

Every single person has a past, some of those pasts being more dramatic than others. I have a lot of angst about parts of my quest to mature, heal, and grow. I have heard people declare; *I wouldn't change anything about my life.*

I have never made that statement; if possible, I would pay a hundred million dollars to buy a few do-overs. Because having a do-over is not possible, I am ready to stand in my truth.

I could argue that the trauma I experienced as a child led to my faulty decision making. But the truth is that some of my choices were based on flawed judgment, period. In writing this book I had to follow the same advice that I offer to my mentees. *It is necessary to push through the mental obstructions, move forward and stop looking backwards.*

As a single parent, I never would have imagined that I would one day have a doctorate, that I would own a significant real estate portfolio, that I would have investment accounts, that I would travel the world, that I would own luxury cars, that I would live in the suburbs, and that I would be a sought-out executive.

I know that my faith in God, my hard work, and my determination is what has led me to where I am today. I never gave up on myself, even in the bleakest times when I almost abandoned my dreams.

I will need to have many discussions with others as a result of writing this book. I believe that I still need to say *I'm sorry* to some people for my behavior. I also need to accept apologies from others for the sake of my own mental and spiritual well-being. I believe that the complete forgiveness that I seek and that I offer will happen in due time.

In today's age of social media, many tools may be used to judge an individual's imperfections. Behind the comfort of a computer screen or a smart phone, people have become the judge, jury, and executioner on Instagram, Facebook, YouTube, and TikTok. Even LinkedIn has now become a breeder of unwelcome opinions. It takes a strong person to block out all the white noise and focus on positivity. I stand firm in accepting who I was in my past and loving myself now.

Whatever you focus on today
should be something that brings you happiness
tomorrow.

CHAPTER THIRTY-SIX

All Things are Working for My Good

My God's love is timely, genuine, and kind.

~ Dr. Marie Brown Mercadel

I am grateful for the blessings that I have been given in my life. On the days when I was unsure how I was going to make it from one day to the next, my faith in God sustained me. Nothing would be possible without my belief that God has a blueprint for me and that my steps have been pre-determined.

From time to time I visit local churches. I enjoy the music, the fellowship, and some of the moving messages from the pulpit. But I know that God's presence is not limited to brick-and-mortar buildings and that he is always present in my heart.

I dislike the hypercritical nature of certain religions, the concept of mega churches, the oratory theatrics, and the financial burden that some churches place on susceptible parishioners. For these reasons, I have focused on practicing my faith in other ways, such as reading bible verses, daily meditation, and silent and spoken prayer.

When I think about my times as a single parent, lying in my bed and staring at the ceiling with less than half of the money that I needed to pay the bills, I know that God had a hand in taking care of me. During the many moments that I was overwhelmed with self-loathing, my prayers to God strengthened me in a way that I am unable to adequately articulate.

When I believed that I wasn't good enough or smart enough, God lined the path for the promotions, the recognition for my work, and my many career ambitions. At times, I have been overcome with emotion when I pray and talk to God. I cry tears of joy when I listen to gospel music because I feel so full of his love, his grace, and his mercy.

I have made mistakes, but God never left me. I am comforted when I speak to God about my fears, and all my worries.

I have always lived by the mantra: *What God has in store for me will be for me.* Whether I applied for a job, pursued a consulting gig, or contemplated a vital life decision, I believed that what was meant for me would be bestowed upon me.

I believe that prayer is powerful, and God will make a way. However, I believe that God wants each of us to do the necessary work within ourselves to succeed. Prayer must be accompanied by actions and sound decisions.

Many individuals have a personal relationship with whatever or whomever they consider to be their higher power. In my case, I believe that God allows people to undergo various tests in life so that they may create their testimony and inspire those who may relate to their problems.

I believe that serving the community for the first half of my life was my primary charge. Today, God has given me the task of using the next phase of my life to promote healing, understanding, and resilience in others. After each of the trials and tribulations in my life, I remain standing. I refused to fall prey to living my life as a victim. I will follow the trail that God has set out for me for with him I know that I will never walk alone.

The trauma of your past
does not define the path
you blaze for your future greatness.

CHAPTER THIRTY-SEVEN

Sole on Fire

Alone we can so do little.
together we can do so much.

~ Helen Keller

Delta Sigma Theta Sorority (DST), Incorporated was established on the campus of Howard University on January 13, 1913, by twenty-two dynamic collegiate women, with an emphasis on promoting academic excellence and providing services to the Black community. The founders of DST were committed to advocating for the equal treatment of Blacks and participated in the historic Suffrage March in 1913 as their first act of public service.

The sorority is the largest public service organization in the world, with a membership of more than three hundred and fifty thousand predominately Black, college-educated women. Today, the sorority is comprised of more than one thousand collegiate and alumnae chapters across the globe. Delta Sigma Theta has established partnerships with other philanthropic entities with common goals, such as Habitat for Humanity, the American Cancer Society, St. Jude Children's Hospital, and the American Heart Association.

During my time as an undergraduate student in 1992, I became aware of the charitable activities of DST and its purpose by attending events that the chapter sponsored in the community and around campus. I was interested in DST's reputation for promoting public service and educational programs. I had the opportunity to work alongside many members of DST and observe their commitment and dedication to public service. However, because of my packed schedule I did not have the wherewithal to pursue my interest in joining a sorority.

In April of 2019, I decided to attend a sorority Rush for college graduates that was held by the North San Diego County Alumnae Chapter (NSDCAC) of DST. A Rush is an informational meeting that permits women the opportunity to learn about the history, background, and admission requirements of the organization. During the meeting, I learned about the Five-Point Programmatic Thrust of DST: Physical and Mental Health, Economic Development, Political Awareness and Involvement, Educational Development, and International Awareness and Involvement.

Having spent all my adult life providing services to defenseless populations, the potential to join DST and work with others to empower members of the community intrigued me. I was invited to join the NSC-DAC and completed a confidential initiation process alongside seven other vibrant women.

Each new class of initiates chooses a line name that is reflective of the women in their group. We chose to identify ourselves as the Eight Indestructible Divas or 8ID. After the line name is chosen, the senior members of DST, referred to as *big sisters* give each initiate a nickname that represents her personality and interests. My nickname *Sole on Fire* was given to me because of my love of designer shoes, those of Christian Louboutin in particular.

Upon joining DST, I volunteered to work as chair of the Economic Development Committee for my local chapter. The initiatives that I spearheaded included teaching a series of financial literacy courses to the Delta Gems, a group of young girls that receive mentoring from members of DST.

My love for motivational speaking is served well by my membership in DST. During my first year, I was honored to deliver the keynote address at the 2020 Founder's Day celebration, an annual event that commemorates the establishment of the sorority. I have also been given the opportunity to participate in panel discussions on a variety of topics and help to shape some of the events that my chapter has sponsored.

In August of 2020, I created the Dr. Marie Brown Mercadel annual scholarship for first-year college students who are majoring in education, social work, nursing, or psychology.

I am delighted to further the mission of DST and join hundreds of like-minded sisters in performing work that is designed to elevate the educational, economic, and political status of Black people.

In my earlier life, I would have doubted that I could build such a strong bond with so many women. Joining the sorority has given me the ability to expand my knowledge about public service, advocacy, and leadership with my Delta sisters.

Trust all of your crazy ideas!
Start each day with
a purposeful direction.

CHAPTER THIRTY-EIGHT

Affirming Me

> *Take as many selfies as you want.*
> *Tell yourself every day that you are enough.*
> *Praise everything about the person*
> *you have become.*
>
> ~ Dr. Marie Brown Mercadel

Five years ago in 2017, I started to surround myself with positive images, motivational passages, and uplifting messages. Any visitor in my home would see signs with positive affirmations on them. Strong. Smart. Confident. Awesome. Amazing. Faith. Belief. Love. Laughter.

In fact, I painted rocks with inspirational messages and placed them throughout my flower garden so that any person who approached my door would be greeted with a cheerful vibe. I believe that people become who they say they are. Therefore, I try to project what I want to be using words that encourage myself and others. Even on the days when I am less hopeful, I may glean energy from my reading uplifting words and notes.

Early on I taught Bryce and Brooklyn to recite positive affirmations every morning when they arise. Their mantra is, *I am strong, I am smart, and I am confident.* I didn't teach them this for them to think that they won't have problems or battles in life. I taught them to recite affirmations so that they may absorb the strength and resolve to address problems head-on.

I will always pour positivity into their soul so that they know that they are loved and valued. The consequences of having them grow up feeling insecure and unloved are too great.

Today, I have an abundance of self-love and take care of myself every day. I am passionate about fitness and carve out time to ride my Peloton bike or run and lift weights each day. I have defined for myself a new love language, cooking, because I enjoy making southern dishes for my family and friends.

On my Instagram and Facebook pages, I have created the hashtag *#Marieisms*. My posts are designed to invoke cheerful and encouraging thoughts for the readers. I reflect on whatever I am going through, hoping to reach those who may not have a voice or the bravery to be transparent in their expressions. However, most of the writings are designed to enrich and elevate my own spirit when I am having a rough day.

Some of my *#Marieisms* are as follows:

- Keep saying it until you believe it.

- You have so much to look forward to that there is no reason to look back.

- You cannot move forward if you continue to re-trace your steps.

- Let the past go, step into your greatness that is just around the corner.

- Tell yourself every single day that you are beautiful and that you are enough.

- Sparkle. Shine. Glow. Flow.

- Know that you are everything you think you are, no matter what "they" say.

- Take Selfies every single day. I love me now more than I ever have in my entire life. What about you? Yes! I AM That Woman!

- With all the TikTok, Facebook, and Instagram illusions of perfect lives and perfect people, don't forget that in real life it is okay to be a regular person who is quietly grinding his or her way to success.

- We were always told to make lemonade out of lemons. The truth of the matter is that it may not always be possible and that things will just plain suck for a time. But, and yes there is a but, resilience is defined as the capacity to recover quickly from difficulties. If you have strong social connections, believe in yourself, and possess the resolve to maintain control of your path, you may come out on the other side of most of the sucky things that you will experience. Trust your instincts. The sun will rise tomorrow.

- Some days you need to look yourself in the eye and proclaim, I am strong, I am smart, I am fabulous, I ROCK, and I am enough. As women, we spend so much time giving much of who we are away and taking care of others that we push taking care of ourselves all the way to the bottom of the priority list. It is a stressful, exhausting, anxiety-provoking, and sometimes thankless role that we play for our family, friends, employers, and others. Every now and then, slow down enough to have a conversation with yourself so that you may be reminded that you are AWESOME.

- If you have ever ridden a bicycle, you know that you must keep peddling forward to stay balanced. Life is the same way. Don't stay stagnant and settle for less because you are afraid to make a change. Be it a change in career, change in a relationship, or a major lifestyle change, pursue the changes flamboyantly and without hesitation. Otherwise, you run the risk of living an unbalanced life filled with regrets, daydreams, and thoughts of what if. Wishing is not enough, doing is required.

- There may be times when you are too much for people. Your brilliance, style, intelligence, and motivation will be intimidating. The way you move, the things you move to, and the things that you refuse to tolerate will make you a target. The fact that you are good, look good, and strive to be better will seem like a foreign concept, and you won't fit into the normal paradigm or status quo. Guess what? That is THEIR problem, don't make it YOURS. Glow as you flow. Keep it moving. Oh, and don't look back because you are not going that way.

- Never apologize for being yourself. Never apologize for being smart. Never apologize for being successful. Never apologize for being ambitious. Never apologize for eliminating toxic things and people from your life. Never apologize for saying yes to yourself and no to others.

- Life doesn't always play out like a game of chess. At times, one must make certain moves to preserve his or her own mental and physical wellness. Don't be afraid to take a detour when you know the time is right.

- Give up the idea of being perfect and being great at everything. Once you are ready to live in your own reality and the truth that is within you, the amazing process of becoming your best self and living your best life may finally happen. Allow yourself to grow stronger through all your imperfections. In doing so, your experiences, both good and bad, may lead to tremendous internal growth. Embrace the daily imperfections. Be uniquely you. Just live, love, and be thankful and grateful.

• Protect your peace. Everyone is not ready to sit at the table with you. In fact, you shouldn't even let some folks stand at the counter.

It has taken me years to find my voice and believe that I am enough. The journey continues, and I am committed to using my platform and my opinions to live my best life and motivate others to do the same. I suggest to each of my mentees that they should create the affirmations that are reflective of who they are and how they want to be viewed. If we start by positively affirming ourselves, we might have the ability to combat our negative expressions.

Make it a point
to uplift someone
and yourself today.

CHAPTER THIRTY-NINE

A Letter to My Teenage Self

> *I am so proud of you, girl.*
> *You are going to be a true rock star.*
> *Hang in there.*
>
> ~ Dr. Marie Brown Mercadel

During the tumultuous times in the life of a teenager, it is difficult to see past the immediacy of whatever is happening in that moment. Often, a slight from a 'friend', facing rejection from a popular boy or girl, or failing to get an invitation to a party held by the most popular person in school feels catastrophic. This is the letter that my 57-year-old self would write today to my teenage self, a shadow of a girl who craved acceptance and was plagued by anxiety and a lack of confidence:

Dear Marie,

I know it seems that you are alone and that there is no one to turn to, but He is always there. Don't worry about those who have bullied you or made fun of you because you appear different. And please do everything you can to keep others from breaking your spirit.

You have lived through a few challenges. Later in life it is likely that you will encounter other unfortunate predicaments. The key will be to stay focused, learn how to walk away from others who do not treat you well, and have faith that what He has in store for you will be yours.

Be kind to yourself. Know and believe that you are special, that you are loved, and that you are a good person. You will shine brightly and accomplish your desire to make a difference in the community by giving your gifts and talents to others.

Some of the people that proclaim to be your friends, and even members of your family, will not root for you or cheer you on. Certain people will decide that they do not care for you without any rational reason. Other people will even pray for you to fail. Sometimes, the ones who hurt you will be the ones who are closest to you, and it will be okay for you to step away and leave them behind.

Individuals will be intimidated by the standards you set for yourself, without understanding that you would offer to help them if they needed it. But it is okay to accept the fact that you are not for everyone.

You are incredible, kind, compassionate, and you will thrive, grow, mature, and help others to do the same. You should know that you matter. The only limitations in your life will be a result of the barriers that you don't step over or knock down. Stand tall.

And by the way, when you get older, there will be these new platforms called Facebook and Instagram. Many of the people from your childhood who picked on you, ignored you, and bullied you will want to be your friend. They will tell you that they are proud of you, and they will be supportive and complimentary. They may even ask you to join their celebrations or ask to be invited to yours.

You will smile, say thank you, and decline their offers. You might also find their behavior oddly gratifying since you know that in part, you were motivated by their cruelty.

You are going to be so amazed by everything you have done in your life. You will lead, you will mentor, you will motivate, and you will inspire others to greatness.

Love Always,
Your future gorgeous, poised, and bold self,

Dr. Marie Brown Mercadel

Know your value,
demand the treatment you deserve,
and don't ever let anyone make you feel
less than enough.

CHAPTER FORTY

Back to My Roots

It's good to know where you came from.
It makes you what you are today.
It's DNA, it's in your blood.

~ Alexander McQueen

Alvin retired from the United States Marine Corps in October of 2016 after thirty years of service. After my tenure at the Urban Corps ended in 2021, we decided to return to North Carolina so that we could live closer to our families. We purchased a home in North Carolina, and Chantell moved as well to about an hour from our house. My sister Mary resides in the family home in Jacksonville, North Carolina, and my brother, Junior, lives nearby.

We are within driving distance of Atlanta and Louisiana and a short flight away from Texas, where most of Alvin's family resides. San Diego will remain the city of my dreams. I loved the tranquility of our neighborhood and our access to the mountains and the ocean, but the worldwide effects of the coronavirus pandemic heightened our desire to spend more time with our family, especially Bryce and Brooklyn.

It is only fitting that I return to the place where I started my career as a public servant to figure out the next phase of my life. As a child and young adult living in North Carolina, my fractured state of mind hindered my ability to initiate the act of healing.

Today, I embrace resilience and the lessons that thriving through adversity has taught me. I endeavor to reach the girls and women that need reassurance that they are *enough*. Through openly speaking my truth, I hope to empower sexual assault victims to fight back and refuse to absorb blame for the actions of another.

From my own experiences, I understand the importance of discussing mental health and making this a priority. The belief that people who suffer from anxiety, depression, or other mental health disorders are *crazy* must be eradicated. Through my work with Delta Sigma Theta Sorority and other community-based organizations, I will continue to do my part to promote emotional well-being and self-care as a top priority.

Real life is not perfect, and neither am I. Gone are the days when I doubted the fact that I am sharp, bold, brilliant, and classy. I am choosing abundance, excellence, faith, and hope as my guiding light. At the risk of sounding cliché, I eagerly anticipate what God has in store for me, and I know that the best is yet to come.

I am affirming me as a badass woman who reeks of Black girl magic and I am enough.

Acknowledgments

To God be the Glory! Without his grace and love my path to healing would have been different. I am mindful that the hands of God carried me through some of my darkest moments.

I wish that my mom Ernestine, my dad Arthur, and my sisters Gwen and Joyce could be here to witness my growth and development. My late sister Gwen sacrificed her life for my siblings and me and raised us as her children. No words of gratitude could ever express how much I owe her for praying for me and boosting me up to become the best version of myself. Thank you to my sister Mary and my brother Arthur Jr. for supporting me.

I am thankful that I have had mentors who poured into me and helped me to mature and flourish in the personal and professional areas of my life. My first mentor, Dr. Alan Ogus, patiently assisted me in learning the clinical methods of delivering behavioral health services and served as a sounding board for ideas on my dissertation. My counselor and friend, Pamela B. Smith, changed the entire course of my career by believing in me, teaching me political acumen, and demonstrating for me how to engage employees. I don't know what she saw in me, but I am thankful that she believed that I could advance the work of the health and human services agency in San Diego.

Thank you to my friend Ellen Schmeding, my pillar of support for the last twenty years. A spiritual soul, she always gave me words of reassurance at the right time.

Thank you to Natalie Robottom, the former Parish President for St. John the Baptist Parish, for giving me the opportunity to serve as the parish chief administrative officer. Unbeknownst to her, she called at the exact right moment and offered me a job while I sat in my car in the State of Louisiana parking garage praying for a miracle that would change my life.

To my line sisters who pledged Delta Sigma Theta Sorority with me and became the Eight Indestructible Divas, Yvette, Taneashia, Glynda, Carol, Darjene', Shanelle, and Vonda, you enriched my life and taught me how to embrace the love of a sisterhood. Each of you means the world to me.

Thank you to my San Diego Black Folks Happy Hour (BFHH) crew, Kimberly, Toroshinia, Harold T., Harold R., Andrew, Kirk, Dorothy, Tooshdi, Adrienne, and Chiara, for inviting me into your lives. Our authentic conversations, the love, the laughter, the honest truths, and the partnership that we had kept me grounded.

I am blessed to have friends who I know would go to the ends of the earth for me, Nancy, Annie, Raven, Traci, Fatou, and Lauren. Altogether, I have one hundred and fifty-five years of friendship with these ladies. They are my sisters, the keepers of my secrets, and my ride-or-die chicks. There is no doubt that any one of them would be on my doorstep with one call. I thank them for embracing the *real* me, even when I was petty, ugly, or unhappy. They have loved me without reservation and expressed joy for my successes.

Thank you to the late Vickie Velasco. We were an odd couple with different backgrounds. We were ebony and ivory. Our age difference spanned twenty-five years. Yet, we understood each other and enjoyed the time that we spent going to the movies, eating at our favorite restaurants, drinking margaritas, and exploring the swamps of Louisiana. Vickie didn't hesitate to tell me if she thought that I had made a mistake, and I could always count on her shoulder to lean on. I know that she is smiling down upon me.

Thank you to Elder and Jackie Nichols, my surrogate parents. You have treated me like your daughter and are always there when I need you. I thank God that my work in San Diego, California, brought us together.

I want to thank my family for loving me. My husband Alvin has given me the room to pursue every crazy idea that I have ever had, whether pursuing multiple degrees and certifications, launching a consulting business, and staying up all night writing this book, he has never held me back from chasing my dreams. It takes a strong man to be married to an assertive, high-strung, driven perfectionist, but he has managed to make it look easy.

My daughter Chantell has given me so much more than I have given her. From the start, she has been my *why* and my reason for being. Her constant reassurances, and gentle nudges have pushed me along the path to writing about my life. She is an awesome person who inspires me to be better. Bryce and Brooklyn are the light of my world, and they both give me a great deal of happiness. Thank you for bringing these brilliant and funny human beings into the world.

To my bonus daughters – Kiara, Ariana, and Kortlyn, it is my hope that my relationship with each of you continues to develop and strengthen in the future. I look forward to watching you blaze your own trails in life, and I know that you will do so with confidence and determination.

Thank you to my nieces and nephews whom I consider to be my surrogate children. I hope that they are emboldened by my journey. I wish to motivate them to set audacious goals, work hard, and forge their own unique paths. They have all touched my life in so many ways.

*Embrace the beauty
that exists around you
each day.*

About The Author

Dr. Marie Brown Mercadel is a dedicated public servant who has served communities in North Carolina, Texas, California, and Louisiana. Born in Jacksonville, North Carolina, she has traveled throughout the United States supporting her husband, Master Gunnery Sergeant Alvin R. Mercadel Jr., USMC Retired, in his military career.

Dr. Mercadel completed her undergraduate studies at North Carolina Central University in Durham, North Carolina, and her master's degree and doctorate at the University of Phoenix. She also holds certifications in Lean Six Sigma, and Diversity, Equity, and Inclusion.

She resides in North Carolina and is the sole proprietor of Mercadel Consulting Solutions. A certified strengths-based leadership coach; she also provides mentoring, leadership development, and motivational speaking services.

Dr. Marie is a shopping connoisseur and loves to brag about owning more than three hundred pairs of shoes. She enjoys cooking, fashion, gardening, running, weightlifting, and all things Peloton.

For more information, please connect with Dr. Marie at mercadel-consultingsolutions.net, on Instagram at @drmercconsults, and on Twitter at @dr_Marie_speaks.

Photo Gallery

Arthur Brown Sr., (right), age unknown

Ernestine Brown, my mom, age unknown

The Brown family.

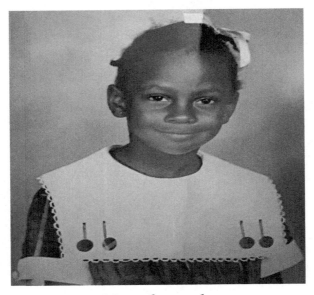

Marie, first grade.

Ernestine Brown, my mom (white dress), in the 1970s.

Ernestine Brown, my mom, in the 1970s.

Marie and Joyce, 1978.

Marie, fifth grade.

My mom and me, Rialto, California, 1981.

My dad and me, Jacksonville, North Carolina, 1986.

My mom, Gwen, Joyce, Junior, Pam, and me, 1992.

Seaworld, 2004, Gwen, Joyce, Mary, Chantell, Misha, Pam, Derrick,
Jalissa, and me.

My sister Gwen, my angel.

A card from Gwen.

185

*The Eight Indestructible Divas
of Delta Sigma Theta Sorority, Incorporated:
Yvette, Taneisha, Glynda, Carol, Vonda, Shanelle, and me.*

Alvin, Chantell, Bryce, Brooklyn, and me, 2019

Bryce, Brooklyn, and me.

Kaminisha, Chantell, Mary, and me.

BFHH Crew, Dorothy, Tory, Tooshdi, Adrienne, Kimberly, and me.

My Besties, Annie, Raven, and Nancy, and me.

Alvin and me, Marine Corps Ball, 2015.

Me with my mentors, Pam and Ellen.

Me with my friend, Vickie Velasco.

Kiara, Alvin, and Ariana.

Finalist, 2020 Business Woman of the Year,
San Diego Woman's Journal.

Chantell and me at my Doctoral graduation,
University of Phoenix Stadium, Phoenix, Arizona, May 2016.

References

Accapadi, M.M. (2007). When white women cry: How white women's tears oppress women of color. *The College Student Affairs Journal,* 26(2).

Ashley, W. (2014). The angry black woman: The impact of pejorative stereotypes on psychotherapy with black women. *Social Work Public Health.* 29, 27-34

Brevata, D.M., Watts, S.A., Keefer, A.L., Madhusudhan, D.K., Taylor, K.T., Clark, D.M., Nelson, R.S., Cokley, K.O., & Hagg, H.K. (2020). Prevalence, predictors, and treatment of impostor syndrome: A systematic review. *Journal of General Internal Medicine,* 35(4), 1252–1275.

Centers for Disease Control and Prevention. (2021). *Adverse Childhood Experiences Prevention Strategy.* Atlanta, GA: National Center for Injury Prevention and Control.

Finkelhor, D., Turner, H.A., Ormrod, R.K., & Hamby, S.L. (2010). Trends in childhood violence and abuse exposure: Evidence from 2 national surveys. *Archives of Pediatric and Adolescent Medicine.*

Fontes, L.A., & Plummer, C. (2010. Cultural issues in disclosures of child sexual abuse. *Journal of Child Sexual Abuse,* 19(5), 491-518.

Hanson, R. F., Resnick, H. S., Saunders, B. E., Kilpatrick, D. G., & Best, C. (1999). Factors related to the reporting of childhood rape. *Child Abuse & Neglect,* 23(6), 559–569.

Hernandez, D. & Rehman, B. (2002). *Colonize this! Young Women of Color on Today's Feminism.* Emeryville: Seal Press.

Hanson, R. F., Kievit, L. W., Saunders, B. E., Smith, D. W., Kilpatrick, D. G., & Resnick, H. S., & Ruggiero, K.J. (2003). Correlates of adolescent reports of sexual assault: Findings from the national survey of adolescents. *Child Maltreatment*, 8(4), 261–272.

Stone, R. (2004). No secrets, no lies: How Black families can heal from sexual abuse. *New York, NY: Harlem Moon.*

Stork, B.R, Akselberg, N.J, Qin, Y, & Miller, D.C. (2020). Adverse Childhood Experiences (ACES) and community physicians: What we've learned. *The Permanente Journal*, 24(19).

U.S. Department of Health and Human Services Administration on Children Youth and Families. (2010). *Child maltreatment.* Washington, DC: U.S. Government Printing Office.

Wyatt, G. E. (1997). *Stolen women: Reclaiming our sexuality and taking back our lives. New York, NY: John Wiley.*

Adverse Childhood Experiences Survey

(re-printed with permission from the CDC public domain)

The Adverse Childhood Experiences Study was conducted by the Centers for Disease Control and Prevention and Kaiser Permanente. The study included seventeen thousand adults and was initiated for the purpose of examining the lifelong impact of traumatic events experienced by children. The data for the survey may be accessed at: cdc.gov/violenceprevention/aces.

The survey questions are listed below:

While you were growing up, during your first eighteen years of life:

1. Did a parent or other adult in the household <u>often</u>:
    Swear at you, insult you, put you down, or humiliate you?
    Or
    Act in a way that made you afraid that you might be physically hurt?

    ☐ Yes ☐ No   If Yes, enter 1 _____

2. Did a parent or other adult in the household often:
    Push, grab, slap, or throw something at you?
    Or
    Ever hit you so hard that you had marks or were injured?

    ☐ Yes ☐ No   If Yes, enter 1 _____

3. Did an adult or a person at least five years older than you ever:

   Touch or fondle you or have you touch their body in a sexual way?

   Or

   Attempt or actually have oral, anal, or vaginal intercourse with you?

   ☐ Yes ☐ No   If Yes, enter 1 _____

4. Did you often feel that:

   No one in your family loved you or thought that you were important or special?

   Or

   Your family didn't look out for each other, feel close to each other, or support each other?

   ☐ Yes ☐ No   If Yes, enter 1 _____

5. Did you often feel that:

   You didn't have enough to eat, had to wear dirty clothes, and had no one to protect you?

   Or

   Your parents were too drunk or high to take care of you or take you to the doctor if you needed it?

   ☐ Yes ☐ No   If Yes, enter 1 _____

6. Were your parents ever separated or divorced?

   ☐ Yes ☐ No   If Yes, enter 1 _____

7. Were any of your parents or other adult caregivers often pushed, grabbed, slapped, or had something thrown at them?

   Or

   Sometimes or often kicked, bitten, hit with a fist, or hit with something?

   Or

Ever repeatedly hit over at least a few minutes or threatened with a gun or knife?

☐ Yes ☐ No   If Yes, enter 1 _____

8. Did you live with anyone who was a problem drinker or alcoholic or who used street drugs?

☐ Yes ☐ No   If Yes, enter 1 _____

9. Was a household member depressed or mentally ill, or did a household member attempt suicide?

☐ Yes ☐ No   If Yes, enter 1 _____

10. Did a household member go to prison?

☐ Yes ☐ No   If Yes, enter 1 _____

ACE SCORE (Total Yes Answers): _____

Resources

American Psychological Association: A professional organization that promotes the health and well-being of members of society by conducting research that addresses substance abuse, violence, and mental and physical health.

www.apa.org

The American Counseling Association: An organization that represents licensed professional counselors, counseling professionals, and counseling students.

www.counseling.org

Black Therapist Rock: A network of Black therapist that provides culturally relevant mental health services that address the lifelong impacts of racial trauma and strives to reduce the sigma related to mental health.

Blacktherapistrock.com

Cerebral: Expert help to manage anxiety, depression, and other mental health disorders. The services provided include evaluation and assessment, medication management, and telephone or video sessions with a licensed therapist.

Cerebral.com

MeToo movement: A social movement supporting the goal of eradicating sexual abuse and sexual harassment. Resources are available for survivors to learn how to heal and develop a sense of safety.

www.Metoomvmt.org

National Alliance on Mental Illness: A grassroots behavioral health organization that is committed to improving the lives of the millions of people that are affected by mental illness.

Nami.org

RAINN National Sexual Assault Telephone Hotline: RAINN partners with a network of service providers nationally to prevent sexual violence and offer resources for victims and survivors.

rainn.org

National Suicide Prevention Lifeline: A national network of local crisis centers that provides free and confidential supports to people that are experiencing a suicidal crisis.

suicidepreventionlifeline.org